Getting to Healed

On the Journey to Peace, Self-Love, and Forgiveness

COMPILED BY

Telishia Berry

Cover art by Mel Davis
Edit and layout by Shonell Bacon

ISBN: 979-8-9946251-0-1

For more information, visit Strive Publishing, Striveipg.com.

If you're ready to write your book or be a co-author in one of our upcoming anthologies, please visit: https://courageouswomanmag.com/write-the-book/

Printed in the United States.

CONTENTS

Introduction

Healing Is a Journey...and You Don't Have to Walk It Alone

Healing is not a single moment, a prayer answered overnight, or a finish line you suddenly cross. Healing is a journey, layered, sacred, and deeply personal. And sometimes, the most powerful part of that journey is discovering that you are not alone in it.

Getting to Healed: On the Journey to Peace, Self-Love, and Forgiveness was created for women who are still finding their footing after heartbreak, trauma, betrayal, loss, disappointment, or silence that lasted far too long. These women look strong on the outside but know there are places within them that still ache and need care.

Within these pages, I share my own forgiveness journey along with eighteen other Courageous Women who open their hearts and share their lived truths, not polished for comfort, but offered with honesty, faith, and bravery. These are stories of survival and surrender, pain that shaped them, healing that transformed them, and moments when God met them right in the middle of it.

You will read about silence that screamed, betrayal that cut deep, forgiveness that felt impossible, and faith that had to be rebuilt from the ground up. You will encounter stories of women who were crushed, yet still called; broken, yet not defeated; wounded, yet willing to heal out loud so that someone else might find hope.

Through every chapter, this truth rises again and again: You are not alone, healing is possible, forgiveness is freedom, and your story still has purpose.

This book does not promise easy answers or quick fixes. Instead, it offers companionship on the road to wholeness. It reminds you that healing may come in fragments through prayer, therapy, tears, worship, boundaries, breath, and time. All of it is sacred.

As you turn these pages, you may see your own story reflected back at you. You may feel seen, challenged, comforted, or stirred. Let this book walk with you. Let it remind you that peace is attainable, self-love is necessary, and forgiveness, while not excusing the pain, can unlock freedom in your soul.

Your healing journey matters.
And it is not over.

You are not behind.
You are not broken beyond repair.

You are becoming.
And you are just getting started.

Dr. Telishia Berry

“The thing that tried to break you will one day be the story that sets someone else free.”

Dr. Tracy A. Allen

EXPERIENCE ONE

When Silence Screamed And Heaven Didn't Look Away

One Woman's Story of Trauma, Survival, and Holy Ground Healing

By Dr. Tracy A. Allen

This is not a fairy tale. There are no glittering redemptions tied with satin bows, no clean endings wrapped in feel-good closure.

What you're about to read is jagged, raw truth peeled from the skin—truth that doesn't whisper but wails. It's the kind you only speak in trembling prayers during the midnight hour, when the ache is too deep for language and you're not sure if God is still listening.

I never thought I'd write this. Not because it wasn't worth telling, but because I didn't believe I'd survive long enough to speak it aloud. Shame was buried so deep—the kind that convinces you silence is safer than freedom. The kind that makes you believe your pain is too messy for the altar.

There was once a little girl living inside this grown woman's body. She smiled when she was told, bowed her head during prayer, and learned early how to shrink herself to stay invisible to predators dressed in love.

Her voice was hushed before it ever found its pitch. Her innocence was stolen. Her truth was swallowed. That secret from her girlhood became a ghost that haunted her womanhood, whispered lies into her purpose, and nearly robbed her of her name.

But God.

This is her story.

A Childhood Silenced

I was raised in a house of mirrors where image was everything and truth was exiled.

I smiled at the church pews, shined my shoes, and practiced my "yes ma'am." I earned praise for being polite and put together. But the applause faded when I got home. Behind closed doors, beneath polished floors, the truth sat quietly in the shadows. And I sat with it.

The abuse started where safety was supposed to live—inside my bloodline. It didn't announce itself with violence. It slid in softly, disguised in silence. It whispered, not shouted.

No bruises for the camera. No evidence to hold up in court. Only the invisible ache of innocence stolen and the confusion that rotted me from the inside out.

I had no words for what was happening. I just knew it felt like my fault.

Running into New Battles

So, I joined the military, thinking I could outrun the past. I thought I could muster the strength to erase the memories. But new traumas waited there, dressed in uniforms, cloaked in the chain of command.

A superior I trusted shattered what little safety I had left. The sexual assault. Emotional terror. Betrayal.

Marriage wasn't a rescue either. It became a battleground where love meant submission, and my body was treated like enemy territory. Rough hands. Brutal sex. Rage masked as affection.

The man who vowed to cherish me punished me for surviving. I was beaten, dehumanized, and erased.

Living Hollow

In my childhood home, love was a transaction. Affection came with conditions. Vulnerability was weakness.

I learned how to disappear in plain sight, how to smile to avoid questions, and how to stay small.

Every room I entered—military, motherhood, marriage—echoed with the shame I carried like a second skin.

I looked whole. But I was hollow. I looked accomplished. But I was aching. Every gold star was a mask. Every laugh was a shield.

And yet, I'm still here.

God Interrupted My Cleaning

My awakening didn't happen in a church pew. Not during revival. Not after a powerful sermon.

It came on an ordinary night. No warning. No worship music in the background. I wasn't seeking healing. I wasn't praying. I was cleaning.

And then God showed up.

I opened an old box, the kind you forget until it forces itself into your memory. Inside was a journal. Torn edges. Faded ink.

The truth was too raw for anyone to read—even me.

Each word reached through time and grabbed me by the throat. It was all there: pain I never named, trauma I had swallowed, pieces of myself I had hidden so well I forgot they existed.

Then I couldn't breathe.

The girl who wrote those pages had never been protected, never believed. But she survived. And now she wanted to be seen.

I fell, not gracefully, not quietly. I hit the floor in a collapse years in the making.

This wasn't a cry for help. It was a breaking point.

I wasn't trying to be strong. Or okay. I broke open.

And God came near.

Not as a judge. Not as a distant observer. But as a Father—tender, present, unshaken by my wreckage. He didn't rush me. He didn't shame me. He stayed with me in it.

And when I had nothing left, when I thought I might disappear into the floor, God spoke.

Not through thunder. But through love.

"Now," He said. *"Let Me build you."*

The Fragments of Healing

Healing didn't arrive like a miracle. No fireworks. No dramatic rescue.

It came in fragments. In whispered prayers. In tear-soaked pillows. In moments that felt like survival, not deliverance.

My therapist met the real me—not the polished version, but the wounded woman under the mask. In that room, I peeled back decades of self-protection.

And for the first time, I spoke the truths I had never dared to say aloud.

Each time I named my pain, the shame lost more of its grip. The lies I carried about my worth, my guilt, and my brokenness began to break.

I wrote. I journaled like my life depended on it. I wrote letters to the little girl I once was. I promised I'd never abandon her again.

I worshiped through tears. I cried during songs I couldn't finish.

When nightmares stole my sleep, I let worship music hold me through the night.

I screamed into pillows. I lay in silence on the floor. I grieved in private.

And God called it holy.

What Healing Looked Like

There was no formula. No blueprint. Just raw faith and sacred undoing.

Some days, my only prayer was, *"Help."*

And it was enough.

Because God didn't meet me with judgment. He met me with presence.

Solitude became sacred.

Faith became shelter.

Worship became a weapon.

And little by little, the numbness cracked.

I began to feel again.

Hope again.

Live again.

Owning My Story

I am still standing. Not because the pain vanished. But because God met me in it. He held me through it.

That's what healing looked like. Not perfect. Not pretty. But holy.

I used to believe my voice was too loud. Too messy. Too dangerous.

But now I know: my voice is divine. It carries the breath of God.

Healing taught me that owning your story doesn't destroy you—it sets you free. It delivers you.

It's not about erasing the past. It's about dragging shame into the light and letting God transform it into something sacred.

Sacred Ground

The events of my life don't get to define me. The trauma doesn't get the final word. God does.

Peace isn't the absence of pain. It's the presence of God in the middle of it.

I've stopped waiting for the pain to pass and started recognizing the holy ground beneath my feet.

Because God meets us in the middle of the suffering—not just on the other side.

Forgiveness broke the chains I had wrapped around my soul. It wasn't about excusing what happened. It was about choosing freedom over bitterness. Healing over hiding. Purpose over pain.

And these scars?

There is no shame.

They're proof.

Proof that I lived. That I endured. That I rose.

Surviving says I made it.

Healing shows why.

To the Reader

If you're reading this with tears in your eyes or a lump in your throat, then this chapter is for you.

This is your confirmation.

Your mirror.

Heaven's whisper: *You are not alone.*

If you're still in the mess—keep going.

If healing feels like war, not victory—keep going.

If your past screams louder than your purpose—lean in.

Because the thing that tried to break you will one day be the story that sets someone else free.

You are not too broken.

Not too far gone.

You are becoming.

And God is not done with you.

He's just getting started.

Healing doesn't always come with thunder. Sometimes it comes with breath. With a whisper.

"Get up."

Sometimes healing looks like deciding to try again tomorrow.

Not every step is bold. Not every moment feels holy.

But when you walk with God, even the valley becomes sacred ground.

If you ask me how I made it, I'll tell you:

God met me in the dark. He didn't wait for the light. He didn't yank me out.

He walked me through it. Step by step. Scar by scar.

And I'm still walking.

Amen.

Dr. Tracy A. Allen is a powerhouse of resilience, leadership, and transformation. A retired U.S. Army officer and decorated Bronze Star recipient, Dr. Allen has turned her battles into blessings, building a legacy that uplifts others. With a Ph.D. in Mental Health Counseling and over twenty years of service to her country, she is a fierce advocate for healing, purpose, and empowerment.

As the founder of Tray Luxe Design, she fuses creativity with calling, offering bold, faith-infused products that inspire and speak truth. A three-time breast cancer survivor, published author, entrepreneur, and community leader, Dr. Allen embodies what it means to rise from pain with power.

Her voice, unapologetically strong and spiritually anchored, is a beacon for survivors, dreamers, and warriors alike. Dr. Allen doesn't just speak about overcoming—she lives it. And she is far from finished. Her mission is clear: to build, to heal, and to lead with divine authority. You can learn more about Dr. Allen via IG (@ trayluxe_design), TikTok (trayluxe.design), and her website (www.trayluxedesign.com).

“The years I thought were wasted were not punishment; they were preparation.”

Telishia Berry

Experience Two

Built, Not Broken

How Faith, Forgiveness, and Courage Reclaimed My Life

By Telishia Berry

A Foundation of Faith

I used to believe my greatest strength was endurance. I was born to teenage parents who were not ready to raise a child. They were alive, but they were still growing up themselves. Before I understood what abandonment meant, I was already navigating it. I was loved, but I was not chosen in the way a child longs to be chosen.

My grandparents stepped in and became my covering. They were strong Christians. Prayer was not a ritual in our home. It was oxygen. I learned to pray as a little girl. I learned that God was near. I learned Scripture before I learned how to process my emotions. Their faith became my foundation.

But even with love and faith surrounding me, there was a quiet ache. My mother struggled with drug addiction. My father was absent. I never wanted to carry the stigma of being that child. So I made a decision early. I would become extraordinary.

If my mother battled heroin, I would battle for greatness. If my story began in instability, I would write an ending of excellence. Achievement became my armor. The stage became my escape. Theater gave me applause when life gave me questions. I traveled with off-Broadway productions, chasing a dream of stardom and trying to prove that my beginnings would not define me.

But pain does not disappear because you perform well.

When Endurance Became Self-Betrayal

At 22, I became pregnant. My dream paused. I was angry at myself. I feared I had ruined everything. For a moment, I considered ending the pregnancy, but the foundation my grandparents poured into me would not allow it. Prayer had shaped my conscience. Faith redirected my fear.

That child was not an interruption. He was a calling.

I married his father and went on to have three beautiful daughters. I built the family structure I never experienced. But beneath the surface, I was already carrying abandonment wounds I had never fully addressed.

The marriage was emotionally unhealthy. There was control, insecurity fueled by drugs and alcohol, isolation from friends and dreams. I was discouraged from finishing college and from pursuing entertainment. The girl who once felt limitless slowly began to shrink.

And I stayed. For 22 years. Not because I lacked faith and strength and not because I was afraid of being a single mother of four, of repeating my mother's narrative, of public failure, and of looking abandoned again.

One day, I would realize that endurance had become self-betrayal.

Choosing Peace

I left for good. I returned to my hometown and slept on my mother's couch, the same mother whose life I had spent years trying not to resemble. It was humbling. It was honest. It was necessary.

I did not have much money. I did not have a flawless plan. But I had peace, and peace felt like victory.

From that couch, I began to dream again. When I finally moved into my own apartment, with just thirty dollars in my bank account and the faith my grandparents had planted in me, I made a decision. I would build something that no one could take from me. That was the beginning of *Courageous Woman Magazine.*

That was not luck. That was legacy.

The prayers of my grandparents were still working. The foundation they built was holding me up. The little girl who learned to pray had become the woman who moved by faith.

For 15 years, the magazine has amplified the voices of courageous women around the world. Women who survived. Women who healed. Women who rose.

Honoring the Woman Who Survived

Recently, I found myself facing another pivot. Burnout surfaced. Old fears whispered, you are too late, you are too old, you missed your moment.

And that is when I understood something powerful: I had forgiven my parents. I had forgiven my ex-husband. I had forgiven circumstances.

But I had not forgiven myself.

I had not forgiven myself for staying. For pausing my dreams. For shrinking. For letting fear extend a season longer than necessary.

So I decided to honor her instead.

The woman who stayed was not foolish. She was navigating abandonment wounds while trying to protect her children.

The woman who endured was not weak. She was operating from the tools she had at the time.

The woman who delayed her dreams was not incapable. She was healing in layers.

God does not waste seasons. He prepares us in them.

The years I thought were lost were actually training. They built discernment, resilience, and compassion for women who silently endure.

I forgive myself, the years, the fear, the delay.

You are not late. No, you are layered. You are not weak. No, you are awakening. Forgive yourself, honor the woman who survived, and then become the woman who thrives. This is the real journey to *healed*, and it begins when you stop condemning yourself for surviving and start celebrating yourself for rising.

Dr. Telishia Berry is the CEO of Strive Publishing and founder and editor-in-chief of *Courageous Woman Magazine*, a publication she built from a simple blog into a thriving print and digital platform with faith, determination, and just $30. With more than 14 years in publishing, she has produced over 200 cover stories featuring notable figures such as Vanessa Bell Calloway, Mo'Nique, and Sheryl Lee Ralph. She has helped more than 500 women publish their stories and become bestselling authors.

A dynamic speaker and creative visionary, Telishia empowers women to launch books, products, and purpose-driven brands. With a background in acting and producing off-Broadway plays, she recently appeared on the television series *Double Crossed* and is currently pitching film projects. A two-time pageant titleholder, including Ms. Elite Woman of Achievement and recipient of a Presidential Award, she is a proud mother of four and grandmother of three.

Connect with Dr. Telishia Berry

E-mail: drberry@courageouswomanmag.com

Websites: CourageousWomanMag.com | StriveIPG.com

IG/Facebook: Courageous Woman Magazine

“What I thought was my breaking point became the birthplace of my breakthrough.”

Mikki A. Ealey

EXPERIENCE THREE

Quiet Betrayal

When Friendship Becomes Silence and Silence Becomes Complicity

By Mikki A. Ealey

They laughed together. Shared secrets. Called each other "sister." But beneath the sisterhood was something darker than betrayal that left scars no one could see. In this case, friendship became a prison.

One friend knew her man was abusive. Knew he was dangerous. Yet when he began coercing her best friend, forcing her into silence and sex, she looked away. She excused it. Protected him. Even as he continued to abuse a 12-year-old girl and her friend's teenage cousin under the same roof. This wasn't just silence. It was silencing. Her best friend endured months of assault, with no refuge, no protection, and no voice. In that household, the word *friendship* was used to cover up fear. And the word *love* was used to justify harm.

Mimi was in her early twenties when she and her son moved into her best friend's home in a raggedy part of the Bronx, New York. It was a cute, cozy, private house on a quiet block, but the streets were littered with pimps, pushers, and prostitutes. Mimi was dating a guy who wined and dined her. She thought he was a real estate agent, but his agency was just a cover-up for his drug dealing. He treated Mimi with love and admiration. However, his advances soon turned into coercion. He would corner me when no one was around, his eyes dark with intent, using threats and manipulation to force me into silence and submission. I felt trapped, unable to escape the nightmare that had become my reality. For almost a year, I endured the abuse in silence. Each day felt like an eternity, filled with fear and dread. I was afraid to speak out, fearing that no one would believe me or that it would destroy my friendship. My best friend, who should have been my protector, turned a blind eye. She saw the fear in my eyes but chose to ignore it, excusing her man's behavior and protecting him instead.

My cries for help went unheard, my pleas for safety dismissed. I felt emotionally abandoned and spiritually suffocated, carrying the heavy burden of a secret while watching a child suffer in silence, too. The friendship that once brought me joy had become a prison, and the word *love* was used to justify the harm inflicted upon me. The cost of this silence was too high. It cost me my voice, my safety, and my innocence.

This is what happens when friendship is twisted into a weapon—when the face that smiles at you by day becomes the one that lets harm happen to you by night.

Being silent in a friendship is more than hurt feelings. It's dimming your light so she can shine. It's avoiding topics that matter to you because she dismisses them. It's holding your truth in because every time you speak, she talks over you, corrects you, or laughs at your pain. But in stories like these, it's even more. It's enduring assault while sleeping under the same roof as your best friend.

Breaking the Silence

Many Black women are raised with the unspoken rule *Don't bring shame to the family. Don't snitch. Don't tell.* But silence in the face of violence is not protection. It's participation. It cost me my voice. It cost a child her safety. It cost both of us our innocence. Healing begins when we give ourselves permission to name what happened. Abuse doesn't always come with bruises. We must stop explaining our boundaries. Instead, we must choose ourselves without guilt, grieve the friendship, seek empowerment, live a life of purpose, and never return out of nostalgia. When my former friend tried to have me jumped by a group of women, I ended all those friendships with style and grace and never looked back.

If you've ever felt silenced by someone who called herself your sister, know this: **Your voice is sacred. Your feelings are valid. And you are allowed to heal loudly.** You are not what happened to you. You are not the silence you were forced into. And you are not alone. I no longer recycle pain. I confront it. I cleanse and release it!

Sometimes, the deepest wounds are not from strangers, but from those we trusted most. If you're holding a story too painful to say out loud, know this: **Your healing begins the moment you decide you're worth more than their comfort.**

SPEAK. HEAL. RISE.

Mikki A. Ealey is an inspiring author, Spiritual Life Coach, and proud holder of a paralegal degree. She is the founder and CEO of Mz Social Butterfly Network, LLC, a platform dedicated to empowering women and fostering personal growth. Mikki is also the author of *Ready Set Go: 30 Days of Motivation To Get You To The Next Level* and has contributed to books such as *DIVA Affirmations* and *Courageous Woman.* Her passion lies in helping others unlock their potential, blending encouragement with authenticity.

Connect with Mikki Ealey

Email: mealey4@mzsocialbutterfly.com

IG: @mzsocialbutterflyllc | @letsrisetothenextlevel

TikTok & Lemon8: @mzsocialbutterflyllc

“Sometimes, the wound must be uncovered before the healing can begin.”

Pastor Tylesha Jones

Experience Four

Pulling Back the Bandages

From Rejection to Redemption: A Journey of Identity and Divine Restoration

By Pastor Tylesha Jones

A Childhood Marked by Rejection

When the purpose of something or someone is not understood, abuse becomes an inevitable reality.

I was born into a family of nine siblings: six girls and three boys. I am the middle child. My arrival into the world was marked by a long and strained separation between my father and mother. The very essence of my being carried the weight of doubt and tension. My father's friend once remarked about me, "Mama's baby, Daddy's maybe." The uncertainty surrounding my conception stirred controversy even while I was still in my mother's womb. From the very beginning, I was shrouded in ambiguity.

So much tension surrounded my parents that, at birth, I wasn't even given a name on my birth certificate. It simply read "Baby Girl Jones." I legally named myself at the age of 35, as though reclaiming the identity that was denied to me from the start. As a baby, my mother would place me in the middle of her bed and make jokes about the way I looked. The echoes of her laughter only deepened the sense of rejection. As I grew older, things only worsened. I was the child who was always left behind, left out, even when it came time for meals with my siblings. I remember sitting on the stairs, tears running down my face as the others ate. The ache of being forgotten was unbearable.

One day, when my mother finally heard my sobs, she coldly asked, "Why are you crying?" Through my tears, I replied, "Because you forgot about me." Her words were sharp and piercing when she responded: "A closed mouth doesn't get fed." From that moment onward, I stopped crying. I forced myself to speak up, to find my voice, but it only led to more rejection, more isolation, and more abuse.

But in that silence, I began to learn the bitter truth—when you are not seen, when your voice is disregarded, healing cannot begin. "A broken spirit who can bear?" (Proverbs 18:14). A closed mouth may not get fed, but neither does a broken heart get healed when it is ignored.

Pulling Back the Bandages

In the absence of love and care, we learn to mask our wounds. We pull the bandages tight over the scars and try to function as if we are whole, yet the healing remains distant, elusive. It is only when we begin to pull back the layers, to expose the pain beneath, that true restoration can begin.

Just as God spoke through the prophet Isaiah, offering a balm for the wounds of His people, "He heals the brokenhearted and binds up their wounds" (Psalm 147:3), so too must we dare to uncover our wounds to the Healer. Only then can the process of healing begin, not in silence or in isolation, but in the vulnerability of acknowledging that we are in need.

May we be brave enough to pull back the bandages, to allow the light of healing to touch our scars, and may we find the courage to speak up for the healing that only God can provide.

Needing a Soft Touch but Receiving Brutality

The road to healing was not swift, nor was it smooth. Even after Jesus embraced me, the echoes of my past often whispered in the stillness, pulling at my soul. At times, I found myself wandering, lost in the labyrinth of memories, unsure if I could ever truly rise from the ashes. The shadows of pain still lingered, trying to claim me once more. I wondered if a broken heart like mine could ever fully heal.

But the love of Jesus, His unfathomable, relentless love, began to weave threads of light into the darkness of my heart. His love wasn't the cruel, jagged love I had known. It was gentle, like a soft rain that cleanses and renews. His love didn't see my wounds and turn away; it saw them, touched them, and whispered healing over them. Where rejection once resided, acceptance now flourished. Where shame once dwelled, grace took root.

And slowly, the pieces of my brokenness began to find purpose. The fragments that once felt like irreparable shards were being restored into something beautiful. Jesus didn't just heal me; He transformed me. The pain I carried for so long became the testimony I now share—my deepest wounds, the places of my greatest suffering, became the soil in which my ministry grew. From the ashes of my past, Jesus brought forth life.

From Brokenness to Purpose

I've learned that sometimes the very thing we think disqualifies us—our pain, our brokenness—becomes the vessel through which God pours His greatest grace. Joseph understood this truth when he said to his brothers, "You intended for evil, but God intended it for good to accomplish what is now being done, the saving of many lives" (Genesis 50:20). And so, I have come to see that my story, my scars, hold the power to help others find their way through the darkness.

To you who reads these words, who feels trapped in a storm of sorrow, know this: Jesus sees you. He sees the quiet tears, the silent cries, the hidden pain that no one else understands. He is not repelled by your wounds; He is drawn to them. His touch is gentle, His love is fierce, and He is waiting, ever patient, to hold you in the embrace that will heal your heart.

Healing is not reserved for the perfect or the unbroken. It is for the weary, the wounded, the ones who have been bruised by life's cruel hand. Jesus does not ask you to be whole before He reaches for you; He comes to you in your brokenness. He is the Healer who does not fear the mess, the scars, or the tears.

The journey to restoration is not always quick, but it is always worth it. With Jesus, even the longest road is a path of grace, and every step is a step toward redemption. You are seen. You are loved. You are not forsaken.

So, rise, beloved. Let His healing touch begin. Let the bandages fall away, for His love is the balm that will restore your soul.

Associate Pastor Tylesha Adaeze Jones is under the leadership of Apostle and Pastor Josephine Odinigwe of Miracle Christian Center, where she is the prayer coordinator of the ministry. Committed to a lifestyle of prayer and the word of God, Pastor Tylesha is a true servant in God's Kingdom.

Connect with Pastor Tylesha Jones

Facebook: Tylesha Adaeze Jones

“Forgiveness is freedom.”

Kimberly Jordan

Experience Five

I Am Enough

From "I Am Not Enough" to Unshakable Identity and Freedom

By Kimberly Jordan

The Roots of Pain and the Search for Identity

I am thankful for this anthology assignment. I believe throughout my journey timing and effective communication are the key ingredients to healing and propelling to unlimited heights.

I have made a sound decision through prayer, embracing it's time for me to see what is this unsettling gnawing that keeps my soul from reaching its complete potential. Mentally traveling down the road of uncertainty and buried pain. It's time to unpack the little girl I have kept tucked away for half a century.

I surrender; I am ready to bring you out to talk in-depth, walk in it, hold hands through it, cry for the mother who was a young adult, celebrate the grandmother (Grum) who carried the torch until her daughter (my momma) was mature enough. Welcome, the lil sister who came along, who also didn't have a say in the situation. Pain was introduced to me long before I could articulate the meaning.

Grum had been a Jehovah's Witness ever since I was able to actively run up and down the stairs chasing Doc, my grandparents' dog. Grum made sure I had books from the Kingdom Hall. *My Book Of Bible Stories* was one of my favorites. Praying, cooking, and extending kindness was Grum's daily ritual. I saw Grum making effort to go the extra mile to bring a smile to my curious face. Yet I began to dance with pain of feeling "I AM NOT ENOUGH." I didn't understand why. My first dance with pain aided me in creating a mindset of false realities, which helped me to build a wall created of ILLUSIONS.

Loss, Responsibility, and the Weight of Promises

The most profound realization was understanding that through my early childhood years, I wasn't given key ingredients—time, nurture, and communication—from the woman who gave birth to me. I gave my GRUM the title. I was too young to grasp it was my momma the entire time who fought tirelessly to maintain the crown she wore.

I am not enough carried into my early teenage years. I became angrier as I watched Momma have two more daughters, but I finally accepted the lil sister that arrived sixteen months after me. I needed an outlet from my reality, and sports became my escape. On the court or running up and down the street throwing or catching a football was my breath of fresh air. Both were physical sports, and I felt a sense of being ENOUGH, at least in those moments.

I wanted more for myself. I needed more for me. I played sports in both junior high years also; I played basketball in high school up until my sophomore year. At the beginning of my sophomore year, tragedy touched my three younger sisters, and the trauma impacted my mental stability. Momma was diagnosed with cancer a month after her thirty-third birthday. Five months later, Momma passed. I knew being a WNBA player was possible for me. I found myself doing just enough in school to get by, which led to cutting corners in other areas of my life. I played tug of war, holding too many ropes: a burning desire to be great, dancing silently with the struggle of failure, and succumbing to NOT BEING ENOUGH.

I was losing all around the board, I had no more moves to make, not on the court or in my home life. I personalized our momma's death. Every kid around us still had their momma no matter what went on once the streetlights came on. They all had their momma to go into the house to. Our dad drowned himself in working. My sisters and I were between the ages of eight and sixteen. Being the oldest, I promised Momma before she passed that I would take care of her daughters. A PROMISE, MY PROMISE. I wasn't in any shape nor was I emotionally mature enough to care for my younger sisters, yet I PROMISED.

Choices, Consequences, and the Journey to Freedom

How do I dream for a life with no guidance as to what road I should take? No more fussing, structure, curfews, no more of a woman's presence…and not just any woman…"THE WOMAN WHO CARRIED HER CROWN IN A FASHION THAT STILL HAS MY SOUL YEARNING TO HEAR HER VOICE!"

I figured it out. I'd have a baby, someone I can call my own. I'll give my son everything I longed for, from the young mother that was still searching to find her way. I loved my son's father and dreamed of building a life, family… a dream come true. He was the greatest guy, a knight in shining armor, even mourned my mom's death with me, *for* me. I was too numb and concerned for my three younger sisters to exude a long period of emotions. Silently, I owe him for being present when I needed someone. I had moments to breathe, yet the control from his actions often left me suffocating and drowning from the pain I felt deep within from losing our mom.

I found an escape, an older man that was too old and far more advanced than me. Twenty-seven years older to be exact. Yet his lifestyle captivated my young nineteen-year-old mind. Mesmerized by the money, diamonds, and beautiful cars, I was ready to soar and leave the life I believed was meant for me. Happily ever after by the control freak. I wanted something different, yet I still carried me into every new adventure in hopes I would see different results. I tried drugs with him; that wasn't a catch for me. The lifestyle was my high. I chased it like my next heartbeat depended on it. I was still enslaved by the control freak. He often used our son as his way to corner me. I wasn't strong enough to cut him completely off. I paid him not to be mean to me on any level.

As an ultimate sacrifice, I planned a robbery with the control freak to appease him. I had no idea his intention was to murder the older guy I had been seeing. Instantly feeling completely responsible, I PROMISED, I WOULDN'T EVER TELL. In the same moment, I thought, *Who's going to take care of my three-year-old son?* I was facing the death penalty on my twenty-first birthday.

I PROMISED MOMMA…and broke my promise to her four years later.

I PROMISED THE CONTROL FREAK…and in not telling on him, I was blamed for the murder committed.

I served thirty-five years, five months, and twenty-four days. I have been home three years. I have found myself still struggling, hearing the whispers of not being enough. The fight that burns within, the strength…I have been blessed by Jehovah God, for He carried me, constantly reminded me that I am beyond resilient. His whispers were just enough to keep the light of HOPE flickering. FAITH kept my heart youthful, my soul is kind, and my spirit is bright.

I forgave THE CONTROL FREAK. **How could I? Vengeance is not mine says the LORD**. I understand being mentally and emotionally free is deeper than being physically free.

FORGIVENESS IS FREEDOM. I KNOW I AM MORE THAN ENOUGH.

Born in Cleveland, Ohio, **Kimberly Jordan** graduated from Sinclair Community College in Marysville, Ohio, in December 2022, receiving an Associate of Individualized Study, with Community and Social Services and Social Work Technician concentrations. She is also a cosmetology instructor. In 1987, she was incarcerated at the age of 20. After serving thirty-five years, five months, and twenty-four days, Kimberly has spent the past three years of physical freedom going deeper into her purpose of healing: to walk into her completeness, embrace the unknown, move in willingness, give to others through the journey, and trust God to carry her.

"I Treasure My Do-over."

Connect with Kimberly Jordan

Email: Kim.Jordan4@icloud.com

“Healing, I’ve learned, doesn’t mean forgetting; it means integrating, carrying what matters forward. It means creating space for both love and loss to coexist.”

Gwen Lavender

Experience Six

...Just Trust Me!

The Gifts of Surrender

By Gwen Lavender

I waited for God's answers. I listened to the whispers as they came. I stayed sensitive to the encounters and nudges of each day, trusting the Holy Spirit's guidance.

In November 2024, I had finished the final chapter of my book, *In the Blink of an Eye.* There was nothing left to add and nothing to take away. It was done. Complete. The book had carried the full weight of my grief, and now it was time to release it—both the story, as well as the grief that it had held.

A Vision for Love

At the beginning of every year, I create a vision board centered around a theme.

My 2023 theme was *Inside Story.* On it, I placed the image of a happy couple—me, arm in arm with a man I couldn't yet name. I covered his face. It wasn't time to see it. But I could feel the steady heartbeat of my desire: companionship from the one who shared my faith and would love me for all that I am.

The vision didn't come to life in 2023. But after 11 years of vision boards, I'd learned that some desires take longer to unfold, so I trusted the timing and carried this one with me into the new year.

By January 2024, the theme had shifted: *A New Me.* In bold letters I wrote, *Each day, I write the story of my life.*

This time, the couple on my vision board was walking on the beach, hand in hand into the sunset. I love walks. I love the beach. I love sunsets. It felt closer now, like I was preparing my heart to receive what I'd been quietly praying for.

In my prayer, I carried my vision, silently and steadily. In the stillness of early mornings, with pen and paper within reach, I waited for God's answers. I listened to the whispers as they came. I stayed sensitive to the encounters and nudges of each day, trusting the Holy Spirit's guidance.

And I also did my part. I began to make small but meaningful changes. I let go of routines that no longer served me. I started keeping the doctor's appointments I had postponed. I started stepping beyond my comfort zone. I gave voice to my vision in trusted circles.

I signed up for line dancing classes and joined an all-women's gym called Curves, where I laughed and sweated with strangers who became friends. I hired a makeup artist and a photographer for a professional photo shoot. I drove a red convertible along the coast, wind in my freshly colored red hair. I giggled with my girlfriends as we tried on lipsticks at Nordstrom's in Vancouver (and found my new favorite shade!).

And I finally furnished my living room, which had remained empty since moving back to California two years ago. Bare walls and silence began to bloom with softness, light, and warmth. I wanted my home to reflect the life I was opening myself to.

I was starting to feel happy again.

The Complications of Joy

Still, some days were complicated.

I later learned about the concept of *recovery guilt.* It's a feeling many grievers don't speak of, that sense of shame or hesitation when you start to feel happy again. It's as if joy itself becomes suspicious. As if loving again betrays the person you lost.

In mid-November 2024, I felt a collision of emotions.

My wedding was set for December 12, and my memoir was nearly ready for print. Both were deeply contrasting milestones, set to unfold within the same week.

However, it felt like each moment deserved its own space. I didn't want them to overlap.

I had poured my soul into this memoir about love, loss, and healing. It felt sacred. Publishing it meant sharing my grief with the world. At the same time, I was stepping into a new chapter of joy, companionship, and love.

How could these coexist? How could I speak publicly about heartbreak while privately planning to get married?

I feared that if they happened too close together, both would be diminished. That one or both stories might be seen as inauthentic. And deep down, I worried I wasn't entirely ready to celebrate publicly.

I felt all of it—gratitude, excitement, sadness, shame, doubt, relief, guilt—often at the same time.

I carried that conflict to my trusted journal. As Judith Campbell once said, "*When the heart speaks, take good notes.*"

I asked myself:

- What emotions are surfacing right now?
- Could these two milestones complement each other, rather than compete?
- How might the timing actually reflect something deeper, something meaningful?
- How can I honor both grief and joy in a way that feels true to me?

Slowly, a shift began to take place.

I began to see that the book release and my wedding weren't two competing events at all. In fact, they were two sides of the same transformation. One was about honoring what I had lost. The other, about embracing what I was now ready to receive.

The timing wasn't mismatched at all. In fact, it was poetic. It was layered. It was God's plan.

The joy of finding love again was part of my healing. And perhaps, that was exactly as it was meant to be.

The Gifts of Surrender

Healing, I've learned, doesn't mean forgetting. It means integrating, carrying what matters forward. It means creating space for both love and loss to coexist. And eventually, allowing one to make room for the other.

On December 12, 2024, I received two things in the same breath.

The first was my first printed copy of *In the Blink of an Eye*—a story of grief, resilience, and healing, released into the world.

The second was a new last name. I married Frank that very same day—12/12/24—during the twelve o'clock hour.

My pastor, Kimberlyn J. Jones, said:

> In the Bible, the number 12 is used to symbolize divine order, perfection, authority, and completeness. The vows you made, the rings, and the sealing with a kiss, were an outward show of what God has already worked together in your hearts. In all things, it is God who brought you together, and with your permission, it is God who will hold you together with His love. Love never fails.

When I reflect on that day, I smile to myself, shake my head, and say, "Look what the Lord has done!"

I had feared the overlap—worried that publishing a memoir about loss while preparing for love would dilute both. But in the end, I see now that they belong together. The book carried me through the stormy nights. It was my life vest when I was sinking. And it brought me, step by step, to the shore where Frank was waiting.

I honor that book because it honors the woman I was—the widow still finding her way. And I speak now as the woman I've become—no longer defined by loss but expanded by it.

Both chapters matter.

Both are true.

And both are sacred.

So if you are reading this from inside the ache of loss, please know it won't always feel this heavy. It won't always be this hard. Hold on to your heart's vision and trust the process, even if your head can't see it yet.

You are still writing your story.

And there is hope beyond this page.

"For I know the plans I have for you," declares the Lord, "plans to prosper you and not to harm you, plans to give you hope and a future" (Jeremiah 29:11).

Gwen Lavender is a #1 bestselling author, licensed minister, inspirational speaker, and transition life coach, helping women navigate life's challenges with courage, confidence, and clarity. Her memoir, *In the Blink of an Eye*, hit the #1 Bestseller list on Amazon in the Journaling category. The story continues in book two, coming soon.

Connect with Gwen Lavender

Email: contact@gwenlavender.com

Facebook: Gwen My-dear Lavender

“Forgiveness was no longer optional. It was oxygen for my soul.”

Tikesha Hearn McNulty

Experience Seven

From Prison to Purpose

A Survivor's Story of Betrayal, Buried Truth, and Finding Freedom Through Forgiveness

By Tikesha Hearn McNulty

The Descent Into Betrayal

My forgiveness journey began in the most unexpected place—jail.

I had moved a family member into my home while still married to a man I'd been with for 18 years. Though I thought our marriage was stable, he had become emotionally distant after his mother died, sinking deeper into alcoholism and unemployment. While I worked in corporate leadership, commuting two hours each way—gone from 6 AM to 11 PM—I began to suspect something was wrong.

A fireplace I hadn't used was lit. Ashes. Burnt wood. Receipts in my bed. My ex-husband naked in the loft. I'd ask questions. Everyone said they didn't know. It left my heart pounding and mind racing.

Because of whom they were—my own family—I had no one I could tell. Not the church. Not my pastor. I had always been the one who covered, even when my heart was bleeding out.

Jail: Rage, Darkness, and the Whisper of Jesus

Eventually, it all came to a head. My mind broke. The betrayal overwhelmed me. I was only 95 pounds from stress. I smoked weed I had found, not knowing it was laced with something.

One Saturday, I still took my daughters out like I had promised—even while seeing demonic visions. I ended up in a terrible accident and hit a pole. I thought I had driven them home and then tried to take my own life. But they were still in the car, which I didn't realize until I heard screaming.

I was arrested and tested. The drugs were laced. I was sent to jail and placed in the psych ward. On meds. Locked away. The Bible looked like Greek. My mind spun like a top. And the rage… I had never felt such hatred.

One day, a demon literally tried to enter me. I fought with all I had and fell off the top bunk. It tried to suck the breath out of me. And all I could whisper was *Jesus*.

And as soon as I said His name, breath came rushing back in.

That night, the Lord led me to Philippians 4:4-8:

Rejoice in the Lord always. Again I will say, rejoice!

Your gentleness be known to all men. The Lord is at hand. Be anxious for nothing, but in everything by prayer and supplication, with thanksgiving, let your requests be made known to God; and the peace of God, which surpasses all understanding, will guard your hearts and minds through Christ Jesus. Finally, brethren, whatever things are true, whatever things are noble, whatever things are just, whatever things are pure, whatever things are lovely, whatever things are of good report, if there is any virtue and if there is anything praiseworthy—meditate on these things.

God knew I was losing my mind and gave me the scriptures to restore it. Glory! Hallelujah!

The Revelation: Forgiveness Is a Command and a Choice

I cried out to God: How do I forgive this kind of pain?

And He said, "You don't have to forgive them. But if you don't, I can't forgive you" (Matthew 6:14–15).

I sat there, weighing it, and realized: No one is worth my soul.

I told God, I want to forgive, but I don't know how.

And He promised: If you focus on Me—not the betrayal—I'll teach you to forgive. I'll pour My love into you so you can pour it out on others.

He asked me: Do you love Me more than your feelings?

And I said, YES.

That day began my journey. I learned that forgiveness isn't a one-time act. It's a process. A daily surrender. A command and a calling.

"No one is worth your soul—but God's love is worth your obedience."

Transformation: From Inmate to Forgiveness Coach

In prison, God discipled me in the silence. He rewired me. I began pouring love into other women, helping them rediscover their identity in Christ. Forgiveness became my language. My lifestyle. My legacy.

God turned my pain into purpose. I founded Hope in Hearts, Forgive with Kesha, Trash to Treasure Recycling Centers, and In My Fatherz House Construction Company. I wrote books. Led retreats. Coached people into freedom.

Forgiveness was no longer optional—it was oxygen.

Reflection and Redemption

Forgiveness doesn't excuse the offense—it heals the soul. I had to forgive the ones who betrayed me. I had to forgive myself—for almost losing my daughters, for losing my mind. God redefined me by His Word. I now live as the righteousness of God in Christ. And the most powerful part? That same family member I couldn't face… is now my best friend. We never had a formal apology. But I forgave anyway.

Because forgiveness isn't about them. It's about you and God.

Closing Word: Forgiveness is a Lifestyle

Forgiveness is not easy, but it is necessary. It unlocks the prison door you've been sitting in all along. And the key has always been in your hand. Its name is Jesus. And the door opens with a decision.

Prayer of Release

Abba Father, I give You my pain. I give You my anger. I give You my brokenness. I lay it all down at the foot of the cross. I choose today to forgive—not because they deserve it, but because You asked me to. I release them into Your hands, and I receive Your peace in return. Heal me. Restore me. Use my story for Your glory.

In Jesus' name, Amen.

Tikesha Hearn McNulty is a Forgiveness Coach, author, and founder of Hope in Hearts, Forgive with Kesha, Trash to Treasure Recycling Centers, and In My Fatherz House Construction Company. Her journey from prison to purpose fuels her passion to help others experience lasting freedom through intimacy with God and the transforming grace of forgiveness. She leads retreats, coaches clients into emotional and spiritual freedom, and empowers individuals to live forgiven, purposeful lives.

Connect with Tikesha McNulty

Email: forgivvellc@gmail.com

Website: www.forgivewithkesha.com

Instagram: @iforgivve and @forgivewithkesha

TikTok: @Tikeshahearn

“I told you your mouth was going to get you into trouble!”

Denise Murphy

EXPERIENCE EIGHT

Overcoming My Toxic Life

From Trauma to Truth—One Woman's Journey of Survival, Faith, and Healing

By Denise Murphy

She screamed that message as the heel of the shoe struck my temple. She whirled me around and threw me against the steel frame of the bunk beds. As my body bounced to the floor like a rag doll, the belt buckle brought large welts across my back.

I knew from previous experience that it was useless to try to run, so I covered my face to brace for the rest of the blows. It was hard to tell if she would get tired of pounding her fists on me and stop or get fueled somewhere in her head to find an excuse to keep going. Just as I was thinking that I hadn't said anything unusual, she finished this onslaught with a kick to my middle. This one was over.

It Began When

My mother was 15 and discovered she was pregnant. At first, she swallowed castor oil and other concoctions to get rid of her mistake. Too afraid to try with a hanger, she hid her bulging belly with a girdle. That restriction was brief, but enough to turn my feet inward and put a curve in my spine. Her teenage womb convulsed with strong contractions to push out the contents, but my balled-up body extended the labor and caused her great pain. Her account of that experience was never forgotten, because on every birthday of mine until she passed, she relived the details of how much I had ruined her life.

Where Was God?

My grandmother did not go to a traditional church but instead dabbled in a mixture of spiritual activities. She put water in bottles around the front yard, chicken bones on the back porch, and on Sundays, went to a cathedral-looking place called the Church of Religious Science.

One time, she took me with her and placed me in the kindergarten class. We sat on a deeply piled and plush rug in a semicircle, meditating on how to be peaceful in our minds so we could find God.

The teacher asked if there were any questions. All I wanted to know was if Jesus was already in my heart, did I have to ask Him to go to my mind, and could she please explain where my mind was, so that Jesus wouldn't get lost. I wasn't allowed to go back to the class, and from then on, I had to go to the main service.

Turning Points

That hunger was encouraged at school by my elementary teachers and fueled into a larger flame when I dressed myself and marched around the corner to the community church. I read all the stories in the Old Testament, filled out every answer in the Junior Quarterly, and even sat in the big chair in front to have a Christian experience.

I didn't know Him personally until years later when my orange Vega flipped over the side of the on-ramp on the freeway. I was on my way home from a rally boycotting apartheid and had been involved in events that had led far from Christian conduct.

I saw my life flash in a video, and an image of the Lord gestured for me to return to the scene of the accident. As the crane lifted the car, I stood up without any broken bones or major damage.

Crawling Toward Healing

That divine encounter spearheaded the beginning of my emotional and spiritual healing. The slow process accelerated when I was filled with the fullness of His Spirit two years later. By then, I was in my early twenties and had been living a double life of secret shame and self-destructive habits.

I just wanted the pain from the trauma and survival techniques to stop so I could stop self-medicating with overperformance, perfectionism, and control. The maze of confusion was compounded by generational patterns and soul ties I had formed to fill in the gaps. Since each layer of dysfunction had unique properties, the treatment for each section took on separate actions and emotional shifts.

I believe one of the most complicated and foundational points of the breakthrough was when I had to identify the relationship I had with my mother as abusive. That didn't come easy, and that label just recently surfaced.

I had always kept a journal to chronicle what was happening behind closed doors, and sometimes it would come out in a poem, a testimony, or even in dreams. It was hard to reckon how a primary caregiver could have done such heinous physical and emotional acts and still live with herself.

There were more questions—why did it only happen to me, why didn't someone stop her, why didn't God answer my prayers to stop her? It was discovered later that she had several conditions that affected her body, causing mini-strokes and chemical imbalances.

The revelation was simple: it wasn't all her fault, and she couldn't help it.

Next Steps

My journey to wholeness had been compared to peeling an onion. Each ring unearthed buried memories, inner vows I had made, and cycles of generational behaviors I had copied.

The unraveling has come in some parts through personal and group therapy with Christian counseling. One key point happened during one of those sessions when I made a list of things I had been believing about myself and others and then researched the truth from the Bible.

One of the lessons I also learned was to give myself the place to grieve any loss caused by past trauma. What I discovered was that those perpetrators did not have what it took to repay those owed debts. The bitterness and feeling cheated consumed my reactions.

My freedom came in that area when I prayed and allowed Jesus to take over on their behalf. Now, as I move forward, it is more apparent that old things have passed away and I am becoming new.

Open your mouth, judge righteously, defend the rights of the poor and needy (Proverbs 31:9).

Denise Murphy is an education specialist dedicated to providing students with a supportive learning environment; she is adept at teaching students that God is the center of every life and academic endeavor. She uses her background in speech communication and dramatic interpretation to write skits and presentations that bring biblical content to life. Denise earned an M.Div. in Practical Theology and has been active in urban ministry both locally and internationally. Currently, she mentors individuals to confidently use their authority as believers to access freedom from generational cycles and past trauma. She enjoys spending time with her husband, Ronald, and family.

Connect with Denise Murphy

E-mail: burshell0929@gmail.com

TikTok: @denisemurphy1117

IG: @denise.drew.murphy

“God doesn’t have to remove a thing to defeat it. Sometimes, He shows His power by keeping you in the middle of it.”

Pastor Tracy Palmer

Experience Nine

He Kept Me

An 11-Year Fight, a Tumor That Stayed, and a God Who Never Left

By Pastor Tracy Palmer

I have been fighting cancer for eleven years. Eleven years of appointments, scans, needle sticks, prayers, surgeries, good days, bad days, hope-filled reports, and frightening ones. Eleven years with Stage 3 metastatic lung cancer, a diagnosis meant to intimidate, overwhelm, and silence. But I'm still here. Not because the journey was easy, and not because I never cried, questioned, or hurt… but because God kept me through every single moment.

Cancer didn't just show up one day and leave. It settled in, tried to stake its claim in my body, and forced me into a battle I never asked for. I had to learn how to live while fighting. How to keep going when my strength ran low. How to trust God when I could not trace Him. And how to keep faith alive even when fear tried to suffocate it.

Through it all, my immediate family, my husband, my children, my grandchildren, church family, and some genuine community friends, held me up. Their love became my anchor. Their prayers carried me. Their presence kept me from collapsing under the weight of the diagnosis. I never had to question where they stood; they were with me, and that mattered more than anything.

But as supportive as they were, the journey brought pain from unexpected places.

The Brain Tumor That Could Not Be Removed

Years into my cancer battle, I was hit with another blow: doctors discovered a brain tumor. The scans showed it was sitting in a dangerous place, wrapped around my carotid artery and pressed up against my optic chiasm. It caused me to go peripherally blind and deaf in my left ear. The surgeons were clear, honest, and gentle, but their words still dropped like stones: "We will go in and remove the tumor."

I went into surgery believing I would wake up with the tumor removed. They would do what they could, but the threat would remain. And that reality shook me to my core.

When I woke up after surgery, groggy and hurting, I reached up and saw the bandage across my face. I felt the pain. And I felt the truth: they could not remove the tumor.

Yet the reality was far more complicated. The tumor was too intertwined with vita structures. Too risky to remove. Too close to everything essential for living; blood flow, my eyesight, and my life. The tumor was too intertwined with vital structures. Too risky to move. Too close to everything essential for living: my blood flow, my eyesight, my life.

There I was, eleven years into cancer, now battling something in my brain that could not be taken out. I wanted answers. I wanted healing. I wanted miracles. What I got was a scar, a story, and a tumor that I am having to learn how to live with.

Holding Faith When Anger Took Over

People think healing is peaceful. Sometimes, it is rage first. Sometimes, the hardest part isn't the sickness; it's the emotions that come with it. I was angry.

Angry that I had lung cancer. Angry that it spread. Angry that I had to fight this long. Angry because I live with sarcoidosis, fibromyalgia, completely arthritic in my lower extremities. Pain...Pain...and more Pain.

There were days I did not want to pray. Days when I didn't have the words. Days I sat in silence wondering, "Lord, why do I have to carry this?"

And yet, even in the anger, God stayed present.

I didn't always feel Him, but He was there. I didn't always understand Him, but He was faithful. I didn't always want to be kept… but He kept me anyway.

"The Lord is close to the brokenhearted and saves those who are crushed in spirit" (Psalm 34:18).

This scripture carried me through nights when fear tried to run the show. Even when my heart was heavy, God held me upright.

The Pain of Betrayal While Fighting for My Life

You would think battling cancer for over a decade would make people kinder. More compassionate. More supportive. But instead, I faced betrayal from extended family members; lies, gossip, made-up stories, and twisted words spoken about me while I was literally fighting for my life.

It hurt. Deeply. Not because their words had power, but because they chose cruelty at a time when I needed grace.

But my immediate family shielded me. They never wavered, never stepped back, never sided with anything but truth. Their love reminded me that I wasn't walking through this alone.

God reminded me: "No weapon formed against you shall prosper" (Isaiah 54:17).

The weapons formed. They formed through sickness, through words, through lies, through betrayal. But they did not prosper.

I learned that sometimes God allows certain people to reveal themselves so you know who cannot go with you into your next season.

The Fight to Believe While Living with What Remains

Healing looks different when the thing that threatens you can't be removed. There's a mental battle that comes with waking up every day knowing the tumor is still there. A spiritual battle that comes with trusting God even when you're still carrying what He could have removed. A physical battle that comes with fighting cancer for eleven long years.

But here is what I learned: God doesn't have to remove a thing to defeat it. Sometimes He shows His power by keeping you in the middle of it.

Isaiah 43:2 says, "When you pass through the waters, I will be with you."

I passed through waters that should have drowned me, but they didn't. I walked through fire that should have burned me, but it didn't. I carry a tumor that should have destroyed me, but it didn't.

Because God kept me. Kept my mind stable. Kept my body functioning. Kept my purpose alive. Kept me from breaking under pressure.

He is a keeper, even when you don't want to be kept.

Rising with Purpose

Eleven years of fighting cancer has changed me. The brain surgery changed me. The betrayal changed me. But none of it destroyed me. God rebuilt me, piece by piece. He gave me strength that didn't make sense. Peace that didn't match my diagnosis. Faith that didn't fold under pressure.

I am not the same woman I was before all of this, but I am stronger. Wiser. More aware of my purpose. My story is not just survival; it is a testimony. It is evidence that God still works miracles in ways we can't always see. It is proof that you can live with what should have killed you. It is a reminder that God's keeping power is real.

I am here. Alive. Present. Purposeful. Healed in ways deeper than medicine can measure. And every day I wake up; tumor and all, I know this truth beyond any doubt: God kept me… even when I didn't want to be kept.

Blessings,

Pastor Tracy Palmer

Pastor Tracy Palmer is an author, mentor, family support advocate, and community leader who is passionate about seeing God's people free, whole, and walking in purpose. She is the founder of Tracy Palmer Ministries and several community-focused initiatives, such as The People Community Outreach & Human Services, 5G (Girls & Guys Gathering Glorifying God), Gracious Guidance Coaching, and *The N.O.W. with Tracy* podcast. A cancer overcomer, Pastor Tracy survived an 11-year battle with stage 3 metastatic lung cancer and now lives courageously with a brain tumor. Through her testimony, leadership, and writing, she empowers others to turn pain into purpose and live victoriously in Christ.

Connect with Pastor Tracy Palmer

E-mail: info.tpministries@gmail.com

Website: https://www.tracypalmerministries.com/

Facebook: Palm.Tra and TracyPalmerMinistries

"What am I doing here? I know God loves me. I am a college graduate and business professional. I have common sense. I can think for myself!"

Terolyn Phinsee

Experience Ten

When the Church Fails You

Healing from Spiritual Abuse, Religious Control, and the Courage to Reclaim Your Faith

By Terolyn Phinsee

As a young 22-year-old, single mother and college student, I sought a sense of belonging and sanctuary and a small church. I had recently accepted the Lord into my life and God's plan for salvation through His son Jesus Christ. Hungry for a deeper relationship with Christ, a friend told me about a church that was "unique" that had an outreach ministry. I was elated. I joined and began to raise my daughter in my newfound church.

When Control Replaces Christ

Within three years, I began feeling uncomfortable about the strict rules, which include banning women and girls from wearing pants, a requirement to let the pastor of the church know about who visited our homes, and informing the pastor of absence from church for vacation, work, etc. This was compounded by the pastor telling us as parishioners that we could only hear from God, through him and that God loved him. He even went on to tell us that if we did not believe he was a man of God that we would be cursed.

Being so young, my heart's desire was to please God and honor leadership. I stayed at the church, saddened by the idea of attending service each Sunday. I'd see marriages falling apart and double standards for the pastor's family that exempted them from the rules forced on the congregation.

When the Breaking Point Comes

Word came back to the pastor that my daughter had worn pants to the mall, and he put my daughter out of the church. That was it! I'd had enough. I tried to stay and continued to see so many inconsistencies in the pastor's personal life. When guests visited the church, he would berate them and demand that they stand up and not look at their bibles unless he told them to. The Holy Spirit inside of me was grieved. God is full of love, grace, and mercy.

On the day that I left for good, the pastor had shouted from the pulpit, "You know nothing!" By this time, I'd married, and my husband and youngest daughter had already left the church. It was like a veil or curtain that had lifted from my eyes. I refused to continue to dummy down.

I looked around and said to myself, "What am I doing here? I know God loves me. I am a college graduate and business professional. I have common sense. I can think for myself!"

I left, without looking back.

Finding God Beyond the Trauma

I began Christian counseling because I did not trust church leaders. I also began to study God's word with intention. I found out that the Lord truly loved me. That no man can curse God's children. Unfortunately, there were many people hurt by this pastor's behavior and many never returned to a church.

I found a beautiful church that I have been a member of for over 15 years. I have learned that I have a God-given purpose and that God loves me and my family. I have learned the importance of being like the Bereans; they searched the scriptures to confirm the validity of what is being shared across the pulpit. I also learned the power of prayer and being filled with the Holy Spirit.

A Call for Accountability and Healing

We are to hold spiritual leaders accountable. They are to be men of Godly character. They are not to dishonor their role, commit sexual sin, they are not to use drugs, or alcohol, threaten God's people, steal, or control their congregation. The church is a spiritual hospital, and it should be growing and caring for the needs of its people.

If you are in a church that you know in your heart is not honoring God, take it before the Lord and leave if there is no change. When ministry leadership honors God, the entire congregation is in unity and great miracles occur, homes are strong, marriages are strengthened, and our lives are blessed.

Terolyn Phinsee is a senior software compliance manager. She is certified as an IT Software Asset Manager with the IAITAM, Microsoft Office User Specialist certified, Certified HIPAA Security Specialist, and the former president of IAMCP (International Assoc. Microsoft Channel Partners). Terolyn is the program director for Titus STEAM Preparatory, a community-based 501c3 organization providing technical training to inner-city underserved youth. She is the CEO of Zip & Go Assist, a technology consulting company based in Los Angeles, CA. She will complete her Theology MBA in June 2026.

Connect with Terolyn Phinsee

E-mail: Terolyn@zipandgoassist.com

Website: zipandgoassist.com

“Your ashes are not the end of your story. They’re the beginning of something beautiful.”

Dr. Tiffany Quinn

Experience Eleven

Crushed, but Called: Healing in the Hands of God

One Woman's Journey Through Betrayal, Loss, and the Quiet Rebuilding of Faith and Purpose

By Dr. Tiffany Quinn

I didn't see it coming—not the heartbreak, not the betrayal, and certainly not the unraveling of everything I had poured my life into. I was a wife, a counselor, a woman of faith, and a spiritual leader. People came to me for guidance, for hope. But when grief and loss came for me, when betrayal and disappointment knocked on my door, I wasn't standing with a Bible in my hand. I was crumbling in silence.

My marriage ended, and not just through a legal document—but through a thousand small heartbreaks that had built up over time. There was betrayal. There was grief. There was the weight of the "long goodbye," that slow, silent grief that starts long before the actual loss, especially in the complicated dynamic of a blended family.

Trying to hold everyone together, maintain peace, and meet expectations that weren't always fair left me empty. Even after he was gone, I found myself trying to still "do right" by everyone—his children, mine, our shared responsibilities, our fractured legacies. It's a different kind of grief when you're the one trying to make peace in a war you didn't start. And blended families don't always come with blended healing. There were expectations to fulfill, appearances to maintain, but I was unraveling inside.

The Breaking Point

I reached a breaking point, the kind that makes you question everything you've ever stood on. I sat in silence one day, on the edge of my bed, and said to God, "I can't live like this. I have nothing left." I was exhausted—spiritually, emotionally, physically. My heart was bleeding, and I didn't know how to stop the pain. I had helped others heal from trauma, but now I was drowning in my own. And so, with courage I didn't know I had, I stepped away from everything. I took a full year off work—not because I had the luxury of it, but because I knew that if I didn't, I might not survive in spirit. I had to reclaim my soul.

That year changed me. I made space for stillness, for truth, and for God to meet me outside of roles, titles, and responsibilities. I wept. I slept. I read. I prayed. I journaled. I walked barefoot in the grass. I stopped pretending. I allowed myself to fall apart and discovered that God doesn't just love our wholeness; He meets us in our brokenness.

He healeth the broken in heart, and bindeth up their wounds (Psalm 147:3).

Learning to Breathe Again

In that quiet year, I found something unexpected: mindfulness. I became a certified mindfulness facilitator—not to run from my pain, but to sit with it, breathe through it, and listen to what it had to teach me.

I began to understand that healing doesn't mean rushing past the pain—it means honoring it. Naming it. Letting it move through you instead of burying it.

Through mindfulness, I stopped reacting to life and started responding with intention. I learned how to stay present, how to breathe when triggers surfaced, how to listen to my body when my soul was weary. And I started teaching others how to do the same—because healing isn't something I just wanted to experience; I wanted to multiply it.

The Power of Forgiveness

Forgiveness was a mountain I didn't want to climb, especially in the context of betrayal. But eventually, I realized that forgiveness wasn't letting them off the hook—it was letting myself off the hook. It was releasing myself from the chains of bitterness, from the exhausting weight of resentment. I forgave, not all at once, but piece by piece, prayer by prayer, tear by tear.

And I forgave myself, too, for not seeing it sooner, for trying to save something that was already lost, for prioritizing peace over my own well-being. That forgiveness set me free.

Healing from the complications of a blended family added a different layer of grief. There were ties I didn't know how to loosen, and roles I didn't know how to exit. People looked to me to be the strong one, the spiritual one. But I had to redefine what strength looked like.

Strength looked like rest. Like boundaries. Like walking away from what was draining me. I had to release the need to be everything to everyone—and choose to be present to myself and to God.

And somewhere in all that silence, in the crushing, I heard God's voice again.

And we know that all things work together for good to them that love God, to them who are the called according to his purpose (Romans 8:28).

From Crushed to Called

God hadn't forgotten me. He was healing me. Slowly. Deeply. Authentically.

I began to feel the oil flowing from my crushing—the anointing, the clarity, the boldness I had lost. I stopped hiding my scars. I started sharing my story. I realized that women needed to hear this—not the polished version, but the process.

Today, I still serve. I still teach. I still minister. But I do so from a different place. I no longer minister from pressure—I minister from peace. I no longer operate from burnout—I operate from overflow.

Sometimes, when life breaks us open, it's so that we can receive more light.

I'm healing out loud so that others know they're not alone. I'm helping women break through guilt, shame, grief, and bitterness—not just through sermons or sessions, but through breath, presence, and love. I teach them to pause, to feel, to forgive, and to rest. That's what healing looks like for me now.

I am no longer surviving—I am living. Fully. Unapologetically. Authentically.

To the woman who feels like her life has fallen apart: this isn't the end. It's the beginning. God isn't punishing you. He's pressing you—so the oil can flow. Your calling hasn't been canceled; it's being refined.

You are not broken beyond repair. You are being rebuilt—with more grace, more wisdom, more power.

You are crushed, yes. But you are still called.

Dr. Tiffany Quinn is a licensed social worker, certified life coach, and mindfulness facilitator with a doctorate in theology. With over 40 years of community leadership and service, she specializes in helping women heal emotionally and spiritually. She is a dynamic speaker, author, and advocate who empowers others to rise from brokenness and walk boldly in purpose.

Connect with Dr. Tiffany Quinn

E-mail: dr.tjquinn2020@gmail.com

IG: @dr.tiffany_quinn

Facebook: sistazion

“Sometimes, when life breaks us open, it’s so that we can receive more light.”

Dr. Briana Rice

EXPERIENCE TWELVE

Healing with Grace

One Woman's Seven-Year Journey Through Heartbreak, Disability, and Purpose—Anchored in Gratitude and Grace

By Dr. Briana Rice

From the time we are born, we are on a very beautiful human journey. There will be love, there will be loss, heartbreak, illness, and eventually, our journey will come to an end.

A Scientist's Journey Around the World

Throughout my journey, I was blessed to become a young Black scientist and world traveler. Over the course of a decade, I traveled to 43 countries and 26 states to attend medical conferences, on a mission to enhance patient safety worldwide. These travels gave me a profound understanding of different cultures and taught me gratitude in ways I would have never imagined. Science opened up that world for me!

However, my darkest moments gave me the opportunity to reflect and meditate. I learned the importance of grace.

Let's reflect back to 2017, when I found myself in Osaka, Japan, burned out, heartbroken, and spiritually drained. I had planned this trip as a birthday escape, hoping for peace. Instead, I faced one of the most disorienting and painful moments of my life.

Days later, I woke up in Taipei, Taiwan, on my birthday—but still hurting. I picked up a book, *Living Beautifully with Uncertainty and Change*. This book had three vows and discussed the importance of gratitude in the darkest moments. Something inside me stirred. I knew something had to change. I made a quiet but firm commitment: the next year, 2018, would be dedicated to healing. That year, I chose gratitude.

Guided by the teachings of *Living Beautifully with Uncertainty and Change*, I embarked on what I called my "Year of Gratitude." It opened my heart to sound healing, Tantra, and a deeper spiritual awakening. I founded The Love and Light Movement in 2020, without realizing that I was laying the foundation for a radical transformation of both my spirit and soul.

Grace in the Stillness

In 2021, everything changed. I was rear-ended by a semi-truck and suffered a traumatic brain injury. That moment stopped everything. My body was broken. My travel came to a halt. I was forced inward into the kind of journey no plane or passport could ever prepare you for.

It was in that stillness, in the silence of recovery, that I discovered what I had really been seeking all along: grace. Surrendering to the magnitude of my injuries and putting all my energy into years of physical therapy and countless treatments led to a profound spiritual awakening.

It's almost as if, when I thought I lost everything, I realized we must give ourselves grace. Even in the chapters of our story that no one wants to read out loud, Spirit is giving us the road map to help others heal by telling our testimony so that when someone else with your situation comes to you in pain, you can empathize, show them how you overcame, and be a beacon of hope.

I realized this had been a seven-year healing journey that began in Taiwan. In the Bible, seven signifies completion, perfection, and divine order. What began as a search to heal a broken heart in 2017 led me into the discovery of a much deeper truth: that sometimes, when life breaks us open, it's so that we can receive more light.

Purpose Beyond the Pain

Even though I now live with an invisible disability here in 2025, I still dared to dream. I still dare to give myself grace and go as fast as I can and as slow as I must. When an opportunity presented itself to compete in a beauty pageant, I said yes, because it gave me the chance to turn my traumatic brain injury into a purposeful pageant platform. Much to my surprise, I won! Becoming a beauty queen pushed my story in front of a larger audience and paired me with disability advocates who furthered my cause and helped me receive better care.

I did not win because of my disability; I won because I chose to champion others with disabilities. Did you know one in four Americans will experience a disability in their lifetime?

The journey into beauty pageantry taught me how to advocate with grace, even after profound loss. After the sudden passing of my dear friend and public relations manager Justin Bowman, I officially launched "Grace for Your Journey" in his honor. It became my personal platform to speak up, not just for myself, but for those who silently suffer with invisible disabilities and inner battles the world cannot see.

Grace for Your Journey is the title of my pageant platform, but this is not just my story; it's an invitation for you. An invitation to reflect and reset. An invitation to remember that your pain does not cancel your purpose. Sometimes, our deepest wounds are the very places where grace enters.

It is a journey we all take when we are healing, so give yourself grace along your journey.

Love and Light,

Dr. Briana Rice

Amb. Dr. Briana Rice, Bsc. (h.c.) is a developmental biologist, graduate of the University of California, Riverside and Azusa Pacific University, and the reigning Miss US Woman of Achievement Ambassador Queen 2026. She has also received an honorary doctorate for over a decade of nonprofit service in healthcare.

She is an International Ambassador for Happiness, a certified Tantra teacher, and a sound healer and yoga instructor, blending science and spirituality to help others heal, rise.

Briana is also the founder of the Love and Light Movement, where she curates upscale events and retreats; the co-founder of the Blackberry Merlot Wine Festival; and the visionary behind Grace for Your Journey, a platform that empowers women and uplifts the voices of those living with invisible disabilities and chronic health conditions.

As the Riverside Director of the Global Society of Female Entrepreneurs, Briana fosters leadership and community among women in business and helps them reclaim their inner power with grace. Learn more about Dr. Briana Rice at her website www.brianarice.com and on Instagram (IG: @bri_from_the_ie).

"Abuse is the initial blow, trauma prolongs the pain, betrayal deepens the wound, deception hides the truth, and offense becomes the trap."

Shannon Scott

EXPERIENCE THIRTEEN

The Four Daggers of Offense: Abuse, Betrayal, Trauma, and Deception

Exposing the Enemy's Strategy Against the Soul and the Pathway to Freedom

By Shannon Scott

Beloved, I pray that you may prosper in all things and be in good health, just as your soul prospers (3 John 1:2, KJV).

This scripture was specifically selected for this healing project because this is the area of focus—our soul. While many natural kingdoms exist on Earth—the plant kingdom, animal kingdom, marine kingdom, and, of course, the human kingdom—these earthly kingdoms are governed by two spiritual kingdoms: the kingdom of light and the kingdom of darkness. It is between these two realms in which the battle for your soul rages. You are either a citizen of one or the other; a double agent of both kingdoms will not survive.

Track with me; I'm heading somewhere with this. Before we proceed, understanding what the soul is will help clarify our perspective. Refining our understanding of this concept is essential because, currently, we see through a glass darkly, meaning our insight into the spiritual realm is limited or obscured by our Creator for our protection. When we catch glimpses of the spiritual realm, it's described as "like seeing a reflection in a dim mirror." 1st Corinthians 13:12 KJV reminds us, "We see in part."

While covering this definition may seem elementary, it is necessary to sharpen our sight. According to science, the soul embodies our mind, will, and emotions, the battleground where the enemy of our soul seeks control.

"Let the enemy pursue my soul, and overtake it; yea, let him tread down my life upon the earth, and lay mine honour in the dust" (Psalm 7:5 KJV).

"For the enemy has pursued my soul, crushing my life to the ground, making me dwell in darkness" (Psalm 143:3 BSB).

The enemy targets the soul, capturing the mind, manipulating emotions, to bend the will away from God. His strategy involves various spiritual weapons, and I refer to a few of them as The Four Daggers of Offense. Yet, God provides us with weapons and protection, which I will discuss in-depth in my book on spiritual warfare.

In this chapter of *Getting to Healed*, we will briefly explore five interconnected terms: abuse, betrayal, deception, offense, and trauma, to establish a framework from which we will build a solid foundation for understanding and finding a path to freedom. By freedom, I mean healing and deliverance. These daggers are weaponry woven into our lives, causing pain but ultimately serving a purpose.

> *No weapon that is formed against thee shall prosper; and every tongue that shall rise against thee in judgment thou shalt condemn. This is the heritage of the servants of the LORD, and their righteousness is of me, saith the LORD* (Isaiah 54:17 KJV).

These weapons may form, but they will not prosper if you keep your mind stayed on Him (Isaiah 26:3).

To establish a foundational truth, we will define each term. Then, we will explore how they are connected. They are intertwined, forming a web of offense meant to trap you. Finally, we will examine the spiritual aspect of these issues through biblical stories, concluding that God has provided a way of escape. Here's how they connect and intertwine in The Web of Deception. They often appear together in emotional and spiritual cycles, especially in relationships, and each one can amplify the damage caused by the other. Without further ado, let's get into it.

The First Dagger of Offense: Abuse, the Entry Point of Pain

Life has a tendency to break us in unexpected ways. For many people, the pain doesn't come from strangers—it comes from those we trust. Abuse—whether emotional, physical, sexual, verbal, or spiritual—often lies at the root of trauma. It breaches boundaries, distorts identity, and destroys trust. Abuse creates a perfect storm in which betrayal and deception reign.

According to the American Psychological Association, abuse involves harmful, non-consensual conduct used to manipulate another person.[1] Within trusted relationships, it distorts perceptions of oneself, others, and even one's own understanding of God. Abuse is a violation; it leaves deep scars that words can't always express. It often begins subtly—through manipulation, control, or silencing the victim's voice, and over time, it becomes normalized. Abuse is more than just what happened; it's the price you pay—your voice, your confidence, your ability to trust, and the effect on your soul.

Don't be misled or discouraged. God doesn't overlook abuse. He sees every wound and promises restoration. "The thief comes only to steal and kill and destroy. I came that they may have life and have it abundantly" (John 10:10, ESV)[2].

David endured Saul's attacks (1 Samuel 19:9–10 NIV). Pharoah mistreated Israel (Exodus 1:14). Even Jesus was assaulted before crucifixion (Matthew 26:67).

Abuse is the enemy's weapons against destiny, yet God redeems.

The Second Dagger of Offense: Betrayal, the Broken Promise

The second dagger, "the broken promise," involves significant breaches of trust. Betrayal causes moral or emotional conflict, often cutting deeper than most wounds because it comes from someone close to us. The *APA Dictionary of Psychology* defines betrayal as lying, disloyalty, keeping secrets, causing harm, providing inadequate support, and making broken promises, all of which can damage emotional well-being.

Psychologist Jennifer Freyd explains betrayal trauma as the difficulty of processing betrayal when the perpetrator is someone we rely on for safety and trustworthiness.[2] In a spiritual context, betrayal disrupts trust in others and God. Freyd notes, "Betrayal turns love into a weapon, especially when tied to abuse or deception, amplifying trauma."

Scripture gives examples of this. In Genesis 4:8, Abel was killed by his brother Cain. Joseph's brothers sold him (Genesis 37:28). In Psalms 41:9 (NIV), David expressed deep anguish when he cried, "Even my close friend, someone I trusted, one who shared my bread, has turned against me." Judas betrayed Jesus with a kiss for "thirty pieces of silver" (Matthew 26:14-15 NIV).

The Third Dagger of Offense: Trauma, the Silent Echo

Trauma is the soul's response to abuse or betrayal. More than just a memory, It alters how we view God, others, and ourselves. Symptoms can include anxiety, mistrust, and shame. Trauma is not a sign of weak faith. Instead, it requires trust in Jesus for healing.

Scripture shows us that Tamar wept (2 Samuel 13:19), David mourned Absalom (2 Samuel 18:33), Job worshipped after loss (Job 1:20).

"He heals the brokenhearted and binds up their wounds" (Psalm 147:3 NIV).

The Fourth Dagger of Offense: Deception, the Lie Beneath the Surface

Deception is the fabrication of truth. Satan is "the father of lies" (John 8:44, NIV). It ties abuse and betrayal together, making victims question their value and faith. Eve was deceived (Genesis 3:13, NIV). Jacob deceived his father, Isaac (Genesis 27:35, NIV). Ananias and Saphira lied to the Holy Spirit (Acts 5:3, NIV).

Healing begins when lies are exposed: *"You will know the truth, and the truth will set you free"* (John 8:32 NIV).

Now that we have briefly explored these weapons that form against us, let's now understand their purpose in the next chapter.

References

1. American Psychological Association. *Abuse.* APA Dictionary of Psychology. https://dictionary.apa.org/abuse
2. American Psychological Association. *Betrayal.* APA Dictionary of Psychology. https://dictionary.apa.org/betrayal
3. American Psychological Association. APA Dictionary of Psychology. https://dictionary.apa.org/
4. Freyd, Jennifer J. *Betrayal Trauma: The Logic of Forgetting Childhood Abuse.* Harvard University Press, 1996.
5. *The Holy Bible*, English Standard Version (ESV). Crossway Bibles, 2001.
6. *The Holy Bible*, King James Version (KJV – Public Domain)
7. *The Holy Bible*, New International Version (NIV © Biblica, Inc.).

Shannon Scott is a visionary, commercial and residential real estate broker, investor, emerging developer, serial entrepreneur, best-selling author, and an Advocate for Kingdom Business. As an honors graduate of the University of Michigan and recipient of the Elnora Ford and Cheryl Harris Intellectual Excellence Award, she holds certifications in Contract Law from Harvard University and in Real Estate Development and Worldviews in American Religious Diversity from the University of Michigan.

A twice-published academic researcher and seven-time published author, Shannon writes at the intersection of faith, leadership, wealth stewardship, and purpose-driven enterprise. Her work equips readers to steward resources with wisdom, expand vision, and align professional success with divine purpose. Additional titles are forthcoming through 2026.

As the founder of multiple brands advancing Kingdom Business, Shannon blends faith and enterprise with intentional precision. For other publications, collaborative works, and forthcoming releases by Shannon Scott, visit on IG @WizdomPress and ShannonScottAuthor.com.

“Forgiveness does not deny what happened. It releases the debt so the offense no longer controls you.”

Shannon Scott

EXPERIENCE FOURTEEN

Offense: The Coup de Grâce

When Offense Becomes a Weapon, and Forgiveness Wins the War

By Shannon Scott

The End Game

Offense is the endgame of the enemy of our souls' war plan—his Coup de Grâce, his final blow. It's the lingering pain of bitterness, unforgiveness, and division. It's the aftermath of abuse, betrayal, trauma, and deception. Offense is not only an emotional wound but a spiritual snare. It traps victims in torment long after abuse or betrayal ends, opening the door to unforgiveness, potentially severing our connection with God. Offense is the focus of this chapter and the enemy's ultimate objective when deploying The Four Daggers of Offense. To establish context, I will begin with the etymological meaning of 'offense' and trace a personal experience in which I learned a critical life lesson: Take no offense!

The Greek term σκάνδαλον (skandalon)—root of the English "scandal"—meant "trap" or "snare," and it evolved into "scandalum" in Latin and "scandal" in English, signifying disgrace or moral stumbling. From Koine Greek meaning "a trap, snare, or stumbling block." The word passed into Latin as scandalum ("cause of offense, temptation to sin"), then into Old French (escandle), and from there into Middle English as scandal, meaning disgrace, offense, or moral downfall.

Holding onto offense gives the enemy of our souls a foothold.

A Season of Betrayal

The spirit behind betrayal presented itself to me on more than one occasion, all within a couple-year span — not just from a few people, but from a multitude of spirits that were unknowingly knitted together for a common cause, a unified purpose. For a season, I had to step back because I was taken aback by what I thought was my imagination, which I eventually recognized as demonic activity. I suspected it was a spiritual coup, a weapon formed against me, but I didn't know why or for what purpose. At first, I took offense, clapping back with a quickness and at every opportunity, reacting with a natural response to a supernatural situation, feeling offended yet taking pleasure in my clever comebacks. Tit for tat, insult for insult. Explaining myself. Defending myself. Trying to reason with the human vessel through which the opposing spirit manifested itself—the host.

An assortment of confrontational spirits—some subtle—continued to manifest through various encounters with different people. Finally, I caught on and no longer felt offended by the perpetrators (notice the word 'traitor' in 'perpetrators'). Instead, I watched, astonished, at what unfolded before me. Reminiscent of *The Matrix*, where anyone at any moment could morph into Agent Smith, longtime friends and family members became like Judas and Job's friends. In some ways, the experience echoed the 1998 film *Fallen*, where a spirit relentlessly trails Denzel Washington's character, Detective John Hobbs—an ancient, malevolent force that passes from one host to another, even with the slightest touch. The spirit would sing the exact words to a song through several unrelated people in different places, signaling to John Hobbs: different people, different places, same spirit.

Now, slower in response—no clap back; instead: self-examination, silent observation, analysis (sometimes decision-paralysis), praying fervently His Word, listening carefully for His Whisper, while wielding the spiritual weapons of my warfare.

> *For the weapons of our warfare are not carnal, but mighty through God to the pulling down of strongholds; casting down imaginations, and every high thing that exalteth itself against the knowledge of God and bringing into captivity every thought to the obedience of Christ* (2 Corinthians 10:4–5, KJV).

My discernment sharpened, immediately recognizing hosts of strife and hosts of confusion. And this is precisely what your abusers, deceivers, betrayers, and those who traumatize are: they are hosts of spirits, mere vessels through which the enemy of our souls works to derail our destiny. *"The thief cometh not, but for to steal, and to kill, and to destroy: I am come that they might have life, and that they might have it more abundantly"* (John 10:10, KJV).

During this time, God taught me to apply everything I had learned thus far —to refine and implement my skills. As Psalm 144:1 says, *"He trains my hands for war and my fingers for battle."* God doesn't want us to fight in the natural, but to sit at His right hand until He makes our enemies our footstool (Psalm 110:1). Our Lord also promises that He will be an enemy to our enemies. *"But if thou shalt indeed obey His voice, and do all that I speak; then I will be an enemy unto thine enemies, and an adversary unto thine adversaries"* (Exodus 23:22, KJV). It was within this season that God revealed who truly surrounded me.

Betrayal eliminated those who could not accompany me to God's next level. I received confirmation of these odd spiritual occurrences when Taylor Welch, from *The Deep End,* articulated this in his podcast, "The Spirit of Python (divination, spiritual counterfeits, & suffocation)" at the 8:35 time mark. He vividly painted an eerily similar spiritual picture, describing my experience in detail. He explained,

> If you're starting to lose business deals that you should not have lost… if relationships are acting really funny around you and all of a sudden …people who were ride or die are now… slandering you… There's weird stuff afoot… This is not

> normal. Then there is spiritual investiture… involvement around you… and it's usually because you're moving forward in something that's dangerous for them… for the kingdom of darkness.

In other words, God is taking you to the next level on your spiritual journey, and the kingdom of darkness is starting to take notice.

Betrayal can serve as a gateway into your next season. Although painful, it often sets the stage for God's greater plan. Without Judas, there would be no cross, and without the cross, no resurrection. Over time, God shifted my focus from thoughts of revenge to purpose, and those who betrayed me faced their own consequences. As a result, I was left with freedom, creativity, and an ever-increasing anointing in my walk with my Lord.

John Bevere in *The Bait of Satan*, powerfully reminds us: *"An offended heart is a breeding ground for deception."* When offense takes root, it becomes fertile soil for bitterness, confusion, and deception to flourish. Jesus said offenses will come (Luke 17:1). The question is not if but when. Those not grounded in the Word of God are easily ensnared, but when your mind is stayed on Him, you maintain peace, and your discernment sharpens. Offense may come, but it won't trap you. Discernment and forgiveness are vital skills for survival.

Forgiveness does not entail denying the occurrence of past events; rather, it involves releasing the debt, thereby freeing oneself from its control. Scriptural examples depict instances of broken trust and abuse, yet God's Word addresses these realities and provides a pathway to healing. Jesus cautioned that offenses would surely come: *"Things that cause people to stumble are bound to come"* (Luke 17:1, NIV). He further stated, *"Many will be offended, will betray one another, and will hate one another"* (Matthew 24:10, NIV). Offense is a spiritual battle. Nonetheless, Holy Scripture affirms that we are not intended to carry offenses. We are explicitly commanded to forgive. Consequently, forgiveness is the only way out.

Jesus' famous last words on the Cross were, *"Father, forgive them; for they know not what they do"* (Luke 23:34).

Conclusion

In summary, abuse wounds, betrayal deepens, trauma echoes, deception hides, and offense is a snare, part of a larger spiritual battle. These intertwine like tattered threads unraveling our worth, yet God, the Master Weaver, restores and rethreads what the enemy attempted to twist into a tangled mess. Take no offense. This is how we win.

> *And when ye stand praying, forgive, if ye have ought against any: that your Father also which is in heaven may forgive you your trespasses. But if ye do not forgive, neither will your Father which is in heaven forgive your trespasses* (Mark 11:25–26, KJV).

Scripture reminds us that there is nothing new under the sun (Ecclesiastes 1:9). Every mistake that you make in life should serve as a lesson with the Bible as your blueprint. Our souls are continuously troubled by the echoes of a past gone wrong. The enemy of our souls calls us backward, reliving a series of unfortunate events from our history. In contrast, the Ancient of Days has written eternity upon our hearts, calling us continuously forward to a Divine Destiny.

With that said, I will conclude with the same scripture with which I commenced the previous chapter, and that is, *"Beloved, I pray that you may prosper in all things and be in health, just as your soul prospers"* (3 John 1:2).

References

1. Bevere, John. *The Bait of Satan*. Charisma House, 1994.
2. *The Holy Bible*, King James Version (KJV – Public Domain); New International Version (NIV © Biblica, Inc.).
3. Skandalon (σκάνδαλον). See: Liddell, H. G., & Scott, R. (1996). *A Greek-English Lexicon* (9th ed.). Oxford: Clarendon Press.
4. Source: Taylor Welch, The Deep End, "The Spirit of Python (Divination, Spiritual Counterfeits, & Suffocation)," YouTube, 8:35 Time mark. https://youtu.be/RO5ymA6wGKk

“Even broken, I will not be defeated.”

Dr. Nephetina Serrano, Ph.D.

Experience Fifteen

Broken, but Not Defeated

From Violence, Betrayal, and Trauma to Unshakeable Faith and Healing

By Dr. Nephetina L. Serrano, Ph.D.

I wasn't looking for conflict that night, but conflict found me. It was a regular fall night, quiet, cool, nothing out of the ordinary. My niece asked me to ride with her to pick up her daughter, my great-niece.

That's all. I wasn't showing up in ministry mode. I wasn't wearing a clergy collar. I wasn't even thinking about being a counselor that night. I was just Auntie. Just someone who wanted to help and spend a little time with family. I didn't suspect anything would go wrong. The night felt calm, peaceful even, and I remember thinking how nice it was to have a simple moment.

But sometimes, even your presence becomes a threat to people who've already decided who you are, and when you walk with God, even when you're silent, you carry something that rattles the spirits in people who haven't faced their own demons. I had no idea the weight of my presence would provoke such a reaction, nor did I anticipate the intensity of what would come after.

Chaos on the Porch

We pulled up to what we assumed would be a typical handoff. Instead, we were met with a wave of tension, a wall of attitudes, my niece's ex, his new girlfriend, and the mother of his infant child. The air was thick with unspoken words, and I remember feeling a sudden tightening in my chest, as if something inside me knew trouble was coming.

The girlfriend didn't say hello. Didn't ask who we were. Didn't want peace. Her mouth was already loaded, and her fists followed. She lunged off the steps and hit me. Right there. No warning. Now hear me: I've been through a lot in my life, but this one? This was different. Not just because of the hit, but because of who stood there watching. There was a mixture of disbelief, fear, and something else I couldn't quite place in the father's eyes.

And the hardest part? The father didn't stop it. He instead joined in the unwarranted attack. I don't know why. I was in total disbelief. He willingly chose to participate in this attack and didn't protect us. That act of betrayal still stings. It wasn't just physical. It was spiritual, and it left a mark deeper than any bruise or scratch. I realized in that moment that true conflict is never just about the body; it is about the spirit, about the unseen battles that rage in people who don't know how to face their own demons and pain.

I remember thinking in that moment, *Even broken, I will not be defeated.* That phrase anchored me even as my body shook and the chaos swirled around me. That night, in a very real sense, I became Broken, But Not Defeated.

The Place That Was Supposed to Protect

That same night, we headed to the police precinct—because we're women who do things right. We don't retaliate. We report. But walking into that station didn't end the trauma. It escalated it.

Before we could even reach the desk, a group of women burst through, five, maybe more, sent there, I believe, with an assignment from hell. They swarmed us with a level of aggression that was shocking, and in that moment, I felt the world shrink around me.

My husband was there this time, trying to hold some of them off, but one woman slipped through. She came for me like she knew exactly what part of my face she wanted to break, and she did. Her fist landed right between my eyes. My nose cracked. My septum broke. Blood everywhere. Screams. I remember the pregnant woman behind the desk running out, grabbing a roll of paper towels, pressing them against my face to try to stop the bleeding.

Officers rushed out, but by then, it was already done. Four days in the hospital. My face bruised and swollen. My spirit fractured.

Litigation is still impending, and to date, *no one* has been held accountable.

We gave our statements. We followed every instruction. But still, nothing. The officers didn't move with urgency. They didn't press forward with investigation. Weeks went by, and no one followed up. No arrest. No outreach. No accountability. It felt like we were dismissed, like our pain was filed away in a drawer no one planned to open, and that's what hurt the most. Not just what happened to us, but how little they cared to make it right.

Even in that moment, I whispered to myself: "I may be broken, but I will not be defeated." That became a mantra, a lifeline, a truth that I clung to when despair threatened to overtake me.

The City Failed Us

This occurred in the city where I was born and raised. In the City of Brotherly Love and Sisterly Affection. The city I've loved. Served. Prayed for. Poured into.

But that night? There was no love. No affection. No protection. The woman who shattered my nose was never named. Never charged. Never even questioned. Justice didn't come. The sense of abandonment weighed heavily, not only because of the physical injury, but because the system failed to honor its promise to protect.

But I'm still here. There are days I wake up and I still feel that punch, not in my face, but in my chest. In the silence. In the memory. There are moments when I replay the scene and ask, "Why me?" I know what it means to show up in love and be met with hate. And still, I rise. Still, I serve. Still, I believe God sees.

There's a pain that comes from being blindsided, not just physically, but spiritually. You think you're just helping. Just showing up. But sometimes, showing up makes you a target. That's a weight few talk about.

But God knows.

And God covers.

Forgiveness Ain't Pretty

Let's talk about forgiveness because people love to quote it, but they rarely walk it. Forgiveness is not soft. It's not cute. It's not quick. It's daily. Gritty. Hard.

There were days I didn't want to forgive. I wanted someone to pay, but I kept hearing God whisper, "Give it to Me." So, I did. I released it in the car. I released it in the shower. I released it when no one else could see the shaking in my hands. Again and again. Because unforgiveness would've kept me trapped in a moment that almost killed me.

I had to pray for those women. I had to release the ones who broke me. Not because they deserved it, but because I deserved freedom. I also prayed for my niece and for my four-year-old great-niece who watched it all. She was trembling, crying, confused, surrounded by people who may have known her, but still chose violence toward the women who raised her, women they had no reason to hate. That part haunts me the most.

What They Didn't Steal

I've lived through a lot. Some of it too heavy for words. The kind of pain that settles in your bones. I've known what it means to survive deep wounds, abuse, threats, losses, betrayal, and still find a way to pour from an honest place. But through every blow, God preserved what mattered most: my joy.

They didn't steal my worship, they didn't touch my calling, and they sure didn't cancel my covenant. The woman hit my face, but she didn't hit my purpose. Even through all of this, I could say with confidence: I am Broken, But Not Defeated.

How I'm Still Healing

Some days I still feel the weight of it. The tiredness. The questions. The what-ifs. But I talk to God. I lean in, and when I can't say anything else, I whisper, "Thank you for life" because I didn't have to still be here. But I am.

"Trust in the Lord with all your heart and lean not on your own understanding; in all your ways acknowledge Him, and He will direct your paths" (Proverbs 3:5–6).

I don't get it all. But I trust the One who does.

Want to know how I'm making it?

1. I told the truth. Not the polished version. The painful one.
2. I let God handle it. That's not cliché. That's covenant.
3. I got therapy. I still go.

4. I forgave. Even when I didn't feel like it.
5. I stayed in the Word. Let it anchor you when nothing else can.

Healing is not instant. Healing is not neat. Healing is messy, but it is real.

I'm Still Here

I believe God will vindicate me. Not because it's fair. But because He's faithful. The women who did this? I release them into His hands. I pray mercy meets them before judgment does.

Today, I stand in my truth. Scared, but stronger. Shaken, but steady. If you've been hit, betrayed, overlooked, or hurt, I'm here to tell you: Healing is real. I'm not all the way there, but I'm getting to healed, and by the grace of God, so will you.

I am broken, yes, I am Broken, But Not Defeated, and that truth carries me forward every single day.

Dr. Nephetina L. Serrano, Ph.D., The Voice of IMPACT, is a dynamic global influencer uniting faith, business, and purpose. As **The Marriage CEOs**™ co-founder, she mentors leaders to thrive in both life and legacy. A respected authority in Marketplace Ministry and executive leadership, she empowers visionaries to rise, rebuild, and reign with divine excellence. Her presence commands rooms; her message awakens greatness. Dr. Serrano embodies Kingdom leadership at its highest level—transforming hearts, organizations, and cultures through wisdom, authenticity, and impact.

Connect with Dr. Nephetina Serrano

E-mail: contact@drnephetinaserrano.com,

drserranoministries@gmail.com

Website: http://drnephetinaserrano.com

IG, Facebook, and TikTok: @drnephetinaserrano

“I didn’t know that my pain would become a pathway.”

Dr. Donna Spivey

Experience Sixteen

I Didn't Know

When Grief Became the Gateway to Calling and Deeper Faith

By Dr. Donna Spivey

When Loss First Arrived

I didn't know that loss would become one of the greatest turning points of my life. I didn't know that grief would introduce me to God in a way comfort never could. And I certainly didn't know that the pain of losing my siblings would shape my calling, deepen my compassion, and anchor my faith for the rest of my life.

In 1993, I lost my first sibling. At that time, I did not understand grief. I only understood shock and absence. Life continued, but something within me shifted. I did not yet have the language to describe the ache, but I felt the weight of finality. What I did not know then was that this loss would quietly draw me toward the Lord. In my confusion and sorrow, my heart began searching for meaning beyond what this world could offer. I didn't know that my pain would become a pathway.

That first loss cracked my heart open, and in that opening, God began to meet me. I did not come to Him with polished prayers or perfect understanding. I came with questions, tears, and a longing for something steady. Grief became the doorway through which my life began to change.

Grieving with Intention

Years later, in 2016, I experienced loss again. This time, I was serving as a senior pastor. My life was fully committed to God, and my days were filled with ministry and responsibility.

But grief does not check your title before it enters. It does not ask permission. It simply arrives.

This loss carried a different weight. Not because it hurt less, but because I understood more. I understood that grief, if unattended, could either refine you or derail you.

I made a conscious decision that sorrow would not destroy what God had entrusted to me. I refused to allow pain to interrupt my obedience or silence my calling.

That does not mean I ignored my grief. It means I grieved with intention.

I chose not to abandon the work God called me to, even while my heart was healing. I learned that obedience can coexist with sorrow. Faith does not require the absence of pain. It requires the refusal to quit.

There were days when ministry felt heavy. Sermons were preached through tears. Prayers were whispered instead of shouted. Some moments required more faith than words.

Still, I showed up.

Not because I was strong in myself, but because I was anchored in God.

I learned that strength is not the absence of grief. It is the presence of resolve.

Ministry Became My Healing

I committed myself to prayer three times a day on a prayer line where people gathered seeking hope. I uplifted others while trusting God to uphold me. I encouraged those facing loss, sickness, disappointment, and fear.

In lifting them, I found myself lifted. In praying for others to endure, I learned endurance firsthand. I didn't know that ministry itself would become part of my healing.

Loss has a way of shrinking your world and tempting you to retreat, but I chose to remain planted. I chose to believe that what God called me to do did not end because someone I loved was gone.

I chose to believe that purpose outlives pain.

I did not know that grief would introduce me to a deeper dimension of God. I did not know that sorrow would strengthen my obedience. I did not know that loss would sharpen my calling.

But I know now.

I know that God wastes nothing. I know that pain can produce purpose. I know that obedience in sorrow builds unshakable faith.

Loss did not derail me. It refined me.

Grief did not silence me. It anchored me.

And what I once did not know, I now understand: God was with me in every tear, every sermon, every prayer. He was shaping a shepherd who could stand. This is not just my story of loss.

It is my testimony of faith.

Dr. Donna Spivey, a pastor, prayer leader, and servant of God, is committed to encouraging others through faith, resilience, and obedience. She serves as a senior pastor and has dedicated her life to prayer, spiritual growth, and ministering to God's people through life's most challenging seasons. Even through personal loss, Dr. Spivey has remained faithful to the call on her life, continuing to labor, pray, and uplift others. Her journey reflects endurance, compassion, and trust in God's purpose. Through her writing and ministry, Dr. Spivey seeks to inspire healing, strength, and hope, reminding others that God's calling endures beyond loss forever faithfully.

Connect with Dr. Donna Spivey

Website: donnaspiveyministries.com

IG: @dr.donnabspivey

TikTok: @livin.n.harmony

“Yes, the mind is a very safe space; it will keep your secrets from you, at least until you are ready to deal with them and put them away properly and without guilt.”

Lander Stovall

Experience Seventeen

North Street Murdered Who I Was

From Stolen Innocence to Healing, Faith, and Freedom

By Lander Stovall

Crossing the Line

In my disobedience, at age 16, I ventured into uncharted waters. I had been warned not to cross North Street—it was unsafe for someone like me. But I did, and in doing so, I metaphorically murdered a part of myself. The experience was one I struggled to live through.

Young and naïve, I went with a neighborhood friend to see her boyfriend. I truly thought it was just a simple walk, but I was unaware I was stepping into danger. I don't think she even fully understood what would happen to me. I never told anyone except when absolutely necessary.

The House and the Encounter

We entered a house I had never been to before. At first, it seemed friendly, with a few boys playing cards. Her boyfriend soon retreated to another room with my friend, leaving me behind. I stayed, waiting and playing cards, until one boy left.

Alone with a boy I didn't know, he proceeded to assault me. I resisted, but he overpowered me, and I was violated. I was a virgin, and the experience left me in shock. I could not scream. I could only shut my eyes and endure. The shame and fear paralyzed me.

The Silence and Its Consequences

I feared my father discovering what had happened. The stories I had heard about sex didn't match my reality, so I convinced myself that nothing had truly occurred. My embarrassment was overwhelming.

It wasn't until I missed my period that the reality hit. My sisters, who were always in sync with each other, noticed my absence of supplies. When asked, I said I didn't know. One sister investigated further and found my diary hidden in a compartment of the grandfather clock.

Writing as a Shield

My mother gave me a diary for my sixteenth birthday. The gift was like a rite of passage, as my older sisters were given diaries for their sixteenth birthdays, too. I wrote sparingly, almost in code. This was the beginning of my journey into poetry—a way to express and conceal my thoughts. My sister discovered the entry about crossing North Street and immediately informed our older sister, our mother, and grandmother.

I was called into my mother's room and questioned at length. Court was in session. I offered only partial truths. The boy involved was well-known, a popular local who even impersonated James Brown. Despite my silence, my mother read between the lines, and my family acted quickly to protect me, shielding my father from the full truth.

The Decision Made for Me

A plan was hatched that I did not fully agree with: the pregnancy would be terminated. At the time, I was shocked that such measures were even possible. I was later cared for by a family doctor, who treated the situation as a miscarriage.

For years, I wondered about the child—what they would have been like, what contributions they might have made. My mind held onto those "what ifs" for a long time.

Moving Toward Forgiveness

Yes, the mind is a very safe space; it will keep your secrets from you—at least until you are ready to face them and put them away properly, without guilt. Ask God to forgive you and then forgive yourself. My future was still ahead of me. I have forgiven those who made the decisions they thought were best at the time. You can never forgive more than God has forgiven you.

Lander Stovall is a four-time published author and an international and key-note speaker. At Temple of Deliverance Apostolic Ministries, she serves as a pastor and head of the evangelistic team. Lander is currently an independent life and health advisor and CEO of 3N1 Cruise and Travel.

Connect with Lander Stovall

E-mail: lansto@bellsouth.net

Website: landerstoval.com

IG: Lander V Stovall

Facebook: Lander Virdure Stovall

“Sometimes, healing doesn’t come to comfort us; it comes to get our attention.”

Dr. Chidell Watkins

Experience Eighteen

Your SCARS Are Your Strength

What Survival Taught Me About Healing

By Dr. Chidell Watkins

The Body Speaks

Healing often whispers before it demands our attention. I didn't understand that at first. I thought healing would feel gentle—like a sigh of relief or awaited answers. Instead, it arrived as an unavoidable, persistent, and urgent interruption in my life.

My first wake-up call came in December 2021 when I was diagnosed with Covid pneumonia. I didn't believe it because I hadn't heard of this. It became very real when I spent twelve days in the hospital fighting for my life. My oxygen level dropped to 48 percent. My blood pressure fell to a deathly low of 75/42, and I had a blood clot in each lung. I couldn't speak for more than fifteen seconds without coughing uncontrollably. My lungs were labored and struggling to breathe (a basic human function we take for granted), suddenly became hard work. Looking back, I see how being 'strong' drowned out discernment—and how my body escalated its messages when I didn't listen. For the first time, I truly understood how fragile life is—and how quickly it can be taken.

Forced Stillness

Eighteen months later, excruciating pain in my left lower back became impossible to ignore. I reached out to friends asking, "Is this that sciatica y'all be talking about?" My days were filled with tears, screams from shooting pains, and biting pillows to tolerate pain worse than childbearing labor. I went to the emergency room four times that week—twice by ambulance. After countless tests, X-rays, MRIs, ineffective medicines, dismissive medical professionals, and unanswered questions, I was finally admitted to the hospital. Doctors diagnosed me with osteomyelitis—a serious, potentially fatal spinal infection. Hearing "fatal" forced me to confront my situation differently. This wasn't just pain anymore—it was life-threatening. I was no longer negotiating discomfort; I was learning what surrender truly meant. Stillness became mandatory, not optional, and fear sat with me every moment of the day. I later learned that actress Amanda Smith shared this exact experience on The Tamron Hall Show. She spent thirty days in the hospital; I spent sixteen. I could not walk for seven weeks. A walker became my lifeline with fear of if I'd ever walk again.

I was sent home with a PICC line and IV pole. I administered antibiotics to myself daily and home health nurses visited weekly. Life slowed to a pace I had never imagined, forcing me to surrender control, confront fear, and be still! In the stillness, I sat with God asking, "What is happening??" I said, "God, I know this isn't the life You have for me!"

Healing also includes having supportive people in your circle. Some friends brought food, delivered groceries and essentials, and helped out overall. One sister friend picked up prescriptions, food, organized groceries, sat with me, and even offered to help me shower. She told me to set my pride aside and accept help, not out of obligation, but because she cared. She and others reminded me I'd always been there for countless others, and now it was time to receive.

Survival on the Freeway

Just as I was regaining strength, life delivered to me another blow less than a year later!

In August 2024, around 3:00 a.m., I was on the FlixBus traveling on the 10 freeway. We were violently rear-ended. Six weeks later, that same bus allegedly suffered a blown tire near the Phoenix airport around 5:20 a.m. We were thrown from our seats. Debris, luggage, people, and shattered glass were flying everywhere. I landed on the floor, taking cover as objects fell on and around me. I was so scared, I thought the bus was rolling over. Something struck me in my chest and in that moment, I thought I was going to die.

Outside the bus, sitting on the freeway—shaken but alive—I asked God, "What are You trying to tell me?" Later, in the ER, I learned a woman had been ejected from the bus and lost her life. I asked God, "Can Your messages be less painful? These hurt." Survival had been speaking to me for years. I just hadn't been listening.

SCARS

Healing shifted when I realized my body wasn't betraying me—it was protecting me. Every scar marked a moment my body chose survival, even when I didn't know how to choose it for myself. Over time, I began to see my scars differently; no longer reminders of weakness, but evidence of strength. Scars are not the wound—they are proof of healing. Scars do not disqualify you, silence you, or weaken you. They sharpen you. I created an acronym for SCARS that captures my journey:

Stories: Each scar tells a story of survival, not just pain.

Created: Scars are formed through living, enduring, and healing.

Aware Of: Pain taught me to listen to my body, my intuition, and the inner voice

Resilience: True resilience shows up in daily life, small victories, and choosing to keep going even when I didn't feel strong.

Strength: Not the kind that pushes through everything, but the kind that knows when to rest, pause, and move forward with purpose.

Getting to Healed

I am still healing. I am still learning. Forgiveness, peace, and full restoration are ongoing journeys for me. I no longer measure healing by how little I hurt, but by how deeply I listen, how honestly I live, and how intentionally I care for myself.

Getting to healed does not require perfection or closure. Healing is a process. It's a journey. Sometimes healing doesn't come to comfort us; it comes to get our attention.

Survival proved God isn't finished with me. Healing is showing me why. I am scarred, but I'm strong—not in spite of what I survived, but because of it.

Dr. Chidell LaTrice Watkins, honorary doctorate recipient and Presidential Lifetime Achievement Award honoree, is an Amazon best-selling author, international speaker, and empowerment advocate. She founded Girlfriends Connected and Etiquette Plus, serving youth and adults in personal development and life skills. She sits on the advisory board for Special Needs Network (Los Angeles). Using her journey from trauma to triumph, she captivates global audiences—including on a TEDx-style platform—with messages of resilience, courage, and transformation, inspiring others to rise, reclaim their power, and live fully with purpose.

Connect with Dr. Chidell LaTrice Watkins

E-mail: chidellwatkins@gmail.com

Website: chidellspeaks.com

IG: @girlfriendsconnected

“Your ashes are not the end of your story; they’re the beginning of something beautiful.”

Minister
Joanne Williams

Experience Nineteen

Beauty from Ashes

A True Story of Homelessness, Survival, and God's Unfailing Grace

By Minister Joanne Williams

The Bonfire

The night my life went up in flames, I watched from my car as my husband and his drinking buddies lit a bonfire in the backyard. Not just any fire, a full-blown burning of everything I owned. They laughed and drank as they tossed my clothes, my kids' toys, my dishes, my memories into the flames. My life was reduced to smoke and ashes while they cracked open another beer.

At 22, I had bought my first two-bedroom house. I had a decent job working in a factory that made doorknobs and a husband who could barely keep a job due to alcoholism. I made it work—until it didn't. After the foreclosure, he moved into his grandmother's house. I had nowhere to go.

All I had left was a backpack, a regular-sized pillowcase stuffed with a few clothes, and two babies depending on me.

Homeless with Two Children

I was 24 years old, with a four-year-old and a six-month-old. I had no answers. No money. No car. No home.

Just a heart full of pain and arms full of children who needed me to be more than I had the strength to be. I became a homeless woman, a bag woman, a dweller among the garbage dumps.

I thought of my babies. I took them to their great-grandmother's house and asked if they could spend the night. I said I'd be back the next morning. That night turned into many. And every evening, I walked away alone with tears that never seemed to stop falling.

I heard them crying in the night even though I wasn't there. I remembered their pulling upon my breast. I wanted to see them, to hold them, to see how they were growing.

The White Cargo Van

With no shelter of my own, I found it—a rusted, abandoned white cargo van down the street. It was dirty. Cold. But it was someplace to lay my tired, aching head.

Every night, I crawled into that van, laid on the metal floor, and cried out to God. Not with eloquent words—just raw, desperate whispers:

"God, please don't forget me. Watch over my babies. Show me the way."

That van became my hiding place. My prayer closet. My lifeline.

My Daily Walk

Every morning, I packed clean baby clothes in my backpack, washed up at the great-grandmother's house, dressed the kids and myself, and headed out.

Three blocks to the babysitter with a baby in my arms, a diaper bag on my back, and my four-year-old's tiny hand in mine.

Then I walked 16 miles to school. And 16 miles back.

Day after day. No shortcuts. No options. Just determination.

I walked on blistered feet with an empty stomach and a burning faith that this wouldn't be forever.

The Price of a Bed

Eventually, their grandmother let me move in—but it came with a price. I had to share a bed with my husband. I had to meet his demands. Not out of love, but out of survival.

I played the role. Quiet. Compliant. Grateful. But each morning, I rose early, got dressed, and disappeared into the day. I was determined not to die in that space.

A Call from Heaven

Then one night, the house phone rang.

It was a sweet elderly woman from my church. She had been searching for me for months. Somehow—miraculously—she found the number to where I was after contacting various church members, friends, and relatives.

Speaking of relatives, my momma wouldn't help me because she wanted me to keep the marriage together. What the #@%^&! I could go on and on about the fact that I was young, uneducated, and without the protection of my parents.

I knew—if nobody else did—that I had made the wrong choice. You know why? Because I did not stop, think, meditate, deliberate, or get any type of counseling before I said, "I do." Girl, just because there is a man in your life doesn't keep you from a whole bunch of mess.

My Florence Nightingale didn't have money to offer, but she offered something better: prayer. We cried and prayed over the phone that night.

And for the first time in a long time, I felt seen. Someone understood.

God Made a Way

The very next day, a classmate told me about a program called HUD Housing. I applied, and within a month, I had the keys to a brand-new two-bedroom apartment. Rent based on income. A real home.

I stood in that apartment, holding my babies, and I wept—not because I was weak—but because God had finally answered.

Beauty from Ashes

Yes—I got the degree.

Yes—I got the job I had always dreamed of.

Yes—I divorced the man who tried to destroy me.

And yes—I stepped into the life God always intended for me.

I am not what I lost.

I am not what they burned.

I am a woman rebuilt by fire, faith, and the hand of a faithful God.

What I Want You to Know

If you're in a place right now where life feels shattered, I want to tell you something:

You can survive.

You can heal.

You can rise.

If You're Facing Homelessness...

You are not trash.

You are not forgotten.

You are not too far gone.

Ask for help. Be relentless. Use what you have. Don't let shame silence you—you still matter.

Reach out for a sister's hand. Someone who understands. Someone who has been there and is willing to help any way she can.

If You're Going Through Divorce...

God still loves you.

He's not ashamed of you.

He sees what you endured, and He is not done with your story.

In times of pain or loss of significant relationships, we like to tell ourselves, "I don't need no man to be happy." And that's true. One is a whole number! However, we do have a need for male interaction. There is a need for "safe, healthy, and sane" male relationships in your life. We can't live without the boys (smile).

Remember to treasure your whole self. Don't sell yourself cheaply. Let God walk with you through the pain into freedom. You will smile again. Get the counseling—it helps.

If You're Just Trying to Survive...

Keep going.

Breathe. Cry. Pray.

Take one brave step at a time. Just keep putting one foot in front of the other. God sees. God hears. God responds.

Survival doesn't look glamorous. It looks like getting back up when life knocks you down. It looks like whispering, "God, I still believe you have something for me."

And He does.

Final Words

So, if no one else has told you today:

You are not alone.

You are stronger than you think.

You are seen by God.

And you will rise again.

This is not the end. You are just getting started.

Your ashes are not the end of your story; they're the beginning of something beautiful.

Minister Joanne Williams is a Christ-centered leader, Bible teacher, speaker, and author dedicated to empowering others in faith. As host of *The Art of Successful Living Podcast* and founder of *Grace On Display Ministries*, she equips believers to grow spiritually, live purposefully, and walk in truth with Jesus Christ.

She authored the books *My Shade of Lipstick is Red* and *10 Life Lessons from the Life of King David.* Joanne Williams holds a master's degree in biblical studies from Long Beach Christian College and a degree in Business Administration from California State University Dominguez Hills.

Minister Williams currently teaches at New Journey Ministries in Hawthorne, California.

Connect with Minister Joanne Williams

E-mail: joannew229@aol.com

Website: www.grace-on-display-ministries.org

IG: @minister_joanne_williams

Facebook: Joanne Cobbs-Williams

“That was the moment I realized I had to stop abandoning myself.”

Katrenia Wright

Experience Twenty

I Stopped Abandoning Myself

Choosing Boundaries, Forgiveness, and Peace Over Self-Sacrifice

By Katrenia Wright

The Wake-Up Call

I almost lost my life trying to save everyone else. For most of my life, I didn't even know there was a word for what I was. I just knew I felt everything. I absorbed people's pain like oxygen. Their sadness, confusion, and devastation became mine.

I have always been the woman who steps into someone else's shoes and sees life through their eyes. I didn't just understand their pain. I carried it.

Being an empath is a double-edged sword.

Add being a perfection-driven Virgo to the mix, and you get a woman who works tirelessly, plans meticulously, feels responsible for everyone, and struggles to say no. A fixer. A provider. A go-getter.

That was me.

I believed I could fix everything and everyone. Even when my gut screamed no, my mouth still said yes.

Drugs, alcohol, and cigarettes were an easy no.

But when it came to people, that was different.

When My Body Said Enough

One day I woke up and realized something was wrong.

My blood pressure was dangerously high. I was exhausted. I could not sleep. I would wake at 1 a.m. and stare at the ceiling until dawn. I had brain fog and anxiety, and needed medication just to steady my breathing.

My doctor looked at me and said, "If you do not control your stress, your stress will control you. And you could end up with a heart attack or a stroke." Then she added, "All the people you are stressing about will continue living their lives. And you will not be here."

That was the moment I realized I had to stop abandoning myself.

Helping others should never cost me my life.

The Shower Prayer

When I got home, I did what I have always done. I got in the shower and talked to God. I suffer from severe osteoarthritis, so kneeling is not easy. I stand under the hot water and pray. I ask God to wash my worries down the drain. I ask for healing. I ask that the same water cleansing my body would refresh my mind and spirit. Years ago, I asked Him to help me release what did not belong to me. I prayed for my family and friends, but I also asked God to separate me from burdens that were never mine to carry.

That was the beginning.

That was when I stopped abandoning myself for the sake of others.

Learning Boundaries

It is still a daily practice. I am naturally caring and supportive, but I am learning to create boundaries that protect my peace. I am learning to say no without guilt. I am learning to choose myself without apology.

When I started honoring my limits, things shifted. My blood pressure improved. I lost weight. My mind became clearer. But the real breakthrough was not physical. It was mental and spiritual. I learned that it is not selfish to protect your heart, your home, or your mental health.

Peace is priceless.

Forgiveness Begins with Me

Over the years, I have learned that forgiveness starts with yourself. I had to forgive myself for ignoring my intuition, for overextending, and for abandoning my own needs. And I had to forgive others. Not because they deserved it, but because I deserved peace.

Forgiveness is not for them.

It is for me. It allows me to move forward and hold my head high, knowing that I am somebody.

I love life. I love myself. I love my family and my friends. Most of all, I love God.

For me, forgiveness and peace walk hand in hand. It is not always easy. But trusting God makes it possible.

Today, I smile. I have peace. I have joy. I have boundaries, which are one of the greatest acts of self-love you can give yourself.

From My Heart to Yours

If you have ever been betrayed, misused, manipulated, or simply drained dry, take a step back. Get on your knees, or get in the shower like I do, and talk to God. Ask Him to help you release what is not yours. Ask Him to help you forgive. Ask Him to help you choose yourself Then do what I did. Stop abandoning yourself. It may be the greatest gift you ever give yourself.

This is my testimony. My healing began the day I chose myself, set boundaries, and refused to lose me again.

Katrenia Wright is an empath, two-time Amazon bestselling author, and advocate for self-love, forgiveness, and personal boundaries. With decades of experience guiding others while learning to honor her own needs, she teaches that protecting your peace is essential. A devoted mother, grandmother, and follower of God, Katrenia inspires readers to embrace their worth, release what is not theirs, and choose themselves without apology. Her work celebrates resilience, faith, and the power of boundaries as a path to healing, peace, and lasting joy.

Connect with Katrenia Wright

Website: https://katreniawright.info/

IG: @thewrightroad

About Digital Artist Mel Davis

Mel Davis is a self-taught digital artist whose work captures the unseen strength, beauty, and resilience within every person. Through his vibrant and emotionally rich artwork, Mel tells stories of hope, faith, and human connection, transforming digital media into powerful expressions of the soul. Driven by a deep love for people, Mel's creative mission is to highlight the inner light that often goes unnoticed. His art is not just visual—it is spiritual, inspiring, and uplifting. Grounded in a strong faith in God and fueled by his devotion to family, Mel brings balance, purpose, and authenticity into everything he creates. His greatest inspiration comes from his biggest supporters—his mother and family—who continue to encourage him to dream boldly and create fearlessly.

Beyond art, Mel is a successful entrepreneur, co-author of the anthology *The Heart of a Black Man*, motivational speaker, fisherman, and mentor. Whether he is speaking on a stage, mentoring others, or creating digital masterpieces, Mel uses his gifts to encourage people to believe in themselves, pursue their purpose, and walk confidently in their God-given calling.

Mel's journey is proof that passion, faith, and perseverance can turn creativity into impact—and dreams into reality.

Want to support Mel's work? Contact him via his website and e-mail.

www.MellowArts.com

Info@MellowArts.com

ANTHOLOGIES BY STRIVE PUBLISHING

WWW.STRIVEIPG.COM

www.ingramcontent.com/pod-product-compliance
Lightning Source LLC
LaVergne TN
LVHW010920110826
845149LV00013B/2434

* 9 7 9 8 9 9 4 6 2 5 1 0 1 *